To

enjoy your Alaska trip...

ALASKA TRACKS

Ned Rozell

AUTHOR'S NOTE

The stories in this book first appeared in Alaska Magazine from 2001 to 2007 as "Wilderness Adventurer" columns. My thanks to editors Andy Hall and Tim Woody for giving me the job and never refusing to pay a travel bill within Alaska. And for letting me run with the column and take it in more of an autobiographical direction than any of us imagined. My job as a science writer at UAF's Geophysical Institute has also taken me great places, and I'm thankful to scientists for letting me tag along, and to my boss Kathy Berry Bertram for letting me follow my nose.

I have edited the essays to update them and to account for my changing taste in words, but they are largely as they first appeared. Original editors that helped, as part of their job or because they wanted to, include Tim Woody, Luke Smith, Rebecca Luczycki, Jennifer Brice, Andy Sterns, and Kristen Rozell. They all made 'em better.

I took the photographs that accompany the stories, except for: "A beautiful friendship" by Steve Reifenstuhl, "Ten years after" by James Hopkins, "Life in the valley of death" by John Eichelberger, "The restless corner" by Martin Truffer, "Continental Divide" by Dave Atkinson, and "Cool School" by Matt Amash. Graphic artist Melissa Guy designed the front and back covers.

Thanks for picking this book up. These essays represent a good chunk of my time in Alaska, and reading back through them I see how lucky I've been to see as much as I have and with so many people. Grateful, I am.

Ned
www.alaskatracks.com

MAP OF CHAPTERS

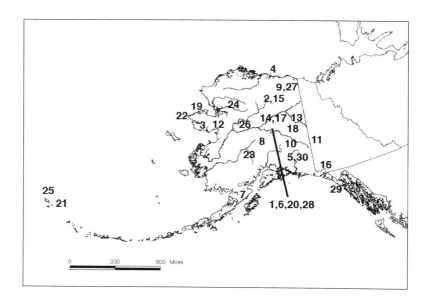

TABLE OF CONTENTS

HOME

"Don't worry," I shouted to Kristen as water curled around boulders ahead of us. "Trust the canoe."

Launching over a small waterfall, we heard the "rrrrrpt" of rocks shaving plastic from my brother's boat. The bow dropped a few feet into fizzing yellow water that feathered over the gunwales and soaked my knees and sneakers.

When the river flattened a few minutes later, I eased my butt back into the seat and relaxed my grip on the paddle. We sat back and watched the passing shoreline, brilliant with leaves colored bronze, lemon yellow, and pumpkin orange.

We were riding New York's Hudson River a few miles from where I lived my first 18 years, taking a breather on a hurried trip back East. My grandmother had died a few days before, after living close to the big river for most of her 98 years. Her last gift was to bring the family together during the fall, a season in New England that Alaska, for all its wonders, cannot match.

As we let the Hudson carry us southward, I thought back to the day 17 years ago when I hugged my parents, said a teary goodbye, and pointed my Ford Courier toward Alaska. Before I drove away, I rolled down the window and said a few dramatic words to my dad:

"I'll be back."

I intended to honor those words, but, to borrow a phrase from Robert Service, I got stuck. Every time I thought about moving away from Alaska, it provided me with an opportunity—a river to ride as a park ranger on the Yukon downstream from Eagle; spruce trees to chainsaw in the Tetlin Hills as a firefighter; rocks to scrub in Prince William Sound after the Exxon Valdez befouled it; moose and sheep flesh to carry for hunting guides; earthquakes, glaciers, volcanoes, and auroras to write about.

I have been lucky to find these jobs, but images of the first woods I first knew and loved have always tugged at me, and the allure of my boyhood home was at its peak as Kristen and I floated the Hudson: it was a sunny, 70-degree day in October, with giant, bushy maples exploding around us in orange and red. When we rushed out of Alaska a few days before, the leaves had fallen and the ground was brown, frozen, and longing for snow. Our Interior fall had lasted about two weeks; it was glorious and rich with yellow aspens and the musk of highbush cranberries, but it barely qualified as a season. The Northeast sets a lovely standard for fall in which the leaves of hardwoods sometimes take months to change from green to orange and the nights are dark, warm, and filled with the din of crickets and other insects that haven't hopped as far north as Alaska.

The presence of my family in the East adds an emotional wallop to its allure. A few yards from the canoe, my brother Drew and his partner Kerri sliced through the water in kayaks. My mom was just a few miles away in an assisted living facility. Five nephews and three nieces who squeal at our arrival live close by, as do their parents, and my two favorite nuns, one of whom is my aunt. Before the trip was over, we would happily put 1,200 miles on Drew's Honda Accord to see all these people.

Along with thoughts of my family, the landscape that formed my first outdoor memories poked at my heart as I twisted the paddle of my brother's canoe. Then we saw the signs.

"Warning. No trespassing, hunting or camping. PCB contamination."

All hometowns have their claim to fame, and mine was the site of a General Electric plant that, along with a GE factory in a neighboring town, had dumped more than 1 million pounds of PCBs (polychlorinated biphenyls) into the Hudson River for 40 years. The resilient, toxic compounds, used by GE in production of capacitors, have settled in the sediments downstream from the factories.

The only contaminants I have tried to avoid on river trips in Alaska are the cysts that cause Giardia. Not that Alaska's rivers are pristine—the effluent from villages in springtime is a big pulse of nastiness—but Alaska doesn't have the grinding history of human settlement that wears on the land, sometimes manifesting itself in the muck of river sandbars.

My brother Drew and I were surprised to see the length of grassy shoreline with PCB warning signs. Though we had both grown to adulthood a few miles off, this was the first time we had ever paddled the river so close to home.

After a mile or so, the PCB signs disappeared and the forest closed back in on the river. As we circled Rogers Island, our take-out point, I scanned the shoreline for potential campsites, more as a habit than a need. The south end of the island, a camping place in the 1750s for Rogers Rangers, the buckskin-clad inventors of guerrilla warfare during the French and Indian War, was now a historical site. A man mowing grass watched us as we paddled by. We could not camp there, but there was a smaller island nearby. As we approached it, I saw a blaze-orange sign tacked to a tree:

"Posted. Private Property. Hunting, Fishing, Trapping, Trespassing for any purpose is strictly forbidden."

I had seen the signs hundreds of times; I'd even helped my father tack up a dozen around our property 40 miles to the north. Except for a limited number of trails, those signs surrounded every chunk of land I knew in upstate New York. And here was another, threatening us with prosecution should we step foot on this forested acre of island.

There, I felt the pangs again, but these were for a sandy willow beach of a remembered island on the Yukon River, where I could float 1,000 miles without seeing a sign that urged me to go away. Sure, maybe I don't own any of the millions of acres of federal and state land in Alaska, but neither does anyone who would exclude me. We share the land up here, we motorheads and leave-no-tracers, sourdoughs and just-transferred airmen. We are not corralled into certain areas to recreate, nor is anyone watching out for our safety in the woods and on the icefields. In a word, we Alaskans are free. Free to take on any outdoor endeavor almost anywhere we please, no matter how noble or stupid.

After long, teary hugs with brothers and sisters and mom and aunt in New York, it was time to endure the stupefying 18 hours of cramped seats and crowded airports that led back to Alaska. Kristen gave me the window seat on the flight from Seattle to Fairbanks. I woke shortly before landing, looked out the window, and loved what I didn't see—beneath the wing was a bumpy landscape where night animals were moving through unbroken corridors of darkness. Above the wing, an arc of aquamarine light glowed to the north as the aurora borealis hung like a halo above northern Alaska. Soon, the airplane tilted into its landing pattern and passed over the white, serpentine outline of the Tanana River. The river flowing through my adopted home is twice the length of New York's Hudson, and so much different.

The lights blinked on in the aircraft cabin. We were home.

NORTHERN DREAM

I had a dream.

Ever since I was a little boy, trailing behind my father as we hiked in New York's Adirondack Mountains, I wanted to live in a place with no pavement. I wanted silence, I wanted trees, I wanted a stream into which I could dip my water bottle without worrying about the people who live upstream.

I have not fulfilled my dream. I live in Fairbanks, the second-largest city in Alaska. I hear the roar of jets overhead as pilots approach Fairbanks International. Tall spruce trees surround the cabin I share with my wife, daughter, and dogs, but my drinking water comes from a coin-operated pump.

I have made a list of the skills and personality traits that enable a person to live in the wilderness, and I have a few of them. Independent worker? Check. Willingness to live without supermarkets, restaurants, and the internal combustion engine? Yup. Ability to kill other creatures without intending to eat them?

I'm stuck on the last one. The wild life often requires the death of something else. Fur trapping is one of the few methods to support oneself while living out there, and the image of snowshoeing a trapline in the golden light of winter fit with my dream, but what about the reality of arriving at a trap with a warm body attached to it?

While hiking a few years ago, I bumped into a trapper who offered to show me the ropes. I accepted, and was soon driving up the Dalton Highway.

I met Brian at his small cluster of buildings in the wide expanse of the Kanuti River valley. He lives 13 miles south of the Arctic Circle, in windy country where spruce trees cling to a table of permafrost, surrounded by streams and tundra potholes that seep into the Kanuti River, which flows to the Koyukuk to the Yukon to the Bering Sea. Looking out from Brian's compound, it is easy to imagine woolly mammoths striding the open tundra, sniffing Pleistocene air.

Brian traps marten, long-bodied, short-legged kin to weasels. Marten live in the spruce groves that stubble the hills behind his home. Feline-quick creatures with ivory claws and needle teeth, marten are abundant but rarely seen. Their appetite for meat, satisfied mostly by voles and shrews, makes them easy to lure. Their fur is smooth and soft, suppler than a beaver's. It takes three marten pelts to make one winter hat.

Brian sets about 100 traps along his 50-mile trapline, which he checks with a snowmachines. The first trap is one-half mile from his home. When he reaches the last trap, he is at the Kanuti River.

Brian loaned me a snowmachine, a Bombardier with an oil-rich fuel mixture. The path to his trapline led us toward Caribou Mountain, a 3,200-foot loaf rising from the flats.

He sped ahead of me in a cloud of blue smoke. I caught up to him 15 minutes later, when he stopped at a trap. He held a strawberry blond marten in front of his chest.

The marten was Brian's first of the one-day-old trapping season. Using his pliers, he tapped its head to knock it out. He then choked the life from a six-pound male. The marten stopped breathing and fell limp. He handed it to me. I held its limp body next to my cheek, feeling its silky warmth in the nine-degree air.

He had harvested 44 marten the previous winter. After he skinned them and groomed their fur, a buyer in Fairbanks gave him an average of $52 dollars for each. That's about $2,300 for a winter's work.

"I average about a marten per mile per season on this trapline," he said, tilting open the seat of his snowmachine and placing the warm body in the cubby. "That's a lot of ground. It takes a lot of country to support these animals."

We wove through forest and crossed treeless open areas where the wind burned our faces pink. Jerking the handlebars over snow-covered tussocks was like wrestling a strong teenager. Alternating my right and left kneecaps on the foam seat, I pulled the machine one way and then the other to avoid tipping. Riding that country was work, not pleasure.

Brian stopped again. As the sun slivered through clouds, he gathered his second marten of the season. The marten's urine stained the snow under the pole set, a spruce pole Brian cut down and wired to a live spruce, providing a ramp for a marten to reach a hunk of meat. Before they reach the bait, which hangs from the end of the pole, marten step on the pan, releasing the stored energy of the trap spring. The trap holds marten by the leg until the trapper arrives to kill it, or until it freezes to death.

Tracks in the snow showed the marten had hopped along like a Slinky in the snow until it got within 10 yards of the bait. From there, the marten left single footprints, trotting to its last meal.

After Brian placed the marten under his seat, I asked him if it bugged him when he killed his first marten.

"Yeah," he said, squishing red meat in a wire loop. "I think I can honestly say I was a little uncomfortable. I don't get a kick out of it.

"I started doing this trapping because, living where I live now, it's another means of getting some income, and it's a reason to get up in the morning."

We continued on through another drainage. Granite tors popped up like stone fingers reaching from the frozen ground. A pair of falcons that should have been in South America rode the wind like kites, eyeing the machines belching smoke below.

On the way home after setting a few dozen traps, Brian drove ahead of me. I followed and watched him stop at a trap. He had a bird in his hands, a gray jay. The jay, a scavenger also known as a camp robber, had wanted a meal of meat. It had the misfortune of hopping on the pan, and the trap amputated a leg. Brian released it, and the bird flew to the top of a black spruce tree, fanning its wings in a failed attempt to keep its balance. While I watched the crippled bird, Brian continued back home.

Alone, I drove the bucking Bombardier over familiar trail, through afternoon sun that hit the tors like a spotlight and stained them orange. As light drained from the sky, movement at one of Brian's traps caught my eye.

I stopped the machine. Another trap had a gray jay, caught by both legs. The bird sat in the trap until I reached at it with a mitten. It beat its wings, fanning my face with a cold breeze.

The jay pecked at me as I peeled its legs from the cold metal jaws. When I released it, the bird flapped to a spruce branch. It centered itself clumsily, and then sat there, broken legs dangling. Puffed like a softball to keep warm, it did not move. I reached out with my mitten to touch its chest. It didn't fly. It didn't peck me anymore. It just looked at me with black marble eyes, with no cries of pain or lament for its approaching death.

Though I knew Brian would want me to, I didn't reset his trap. So far, we had taken as many gray jays as marten. The sparse country in which I stood had already weeded out the fair-weather species, and here I was helping to kill a few of the survivors. I couldn't make sense of that.

As the gray jay watched me straddle the snowmachine, I made my decision. If I am to someday fulfill the dream, it won't be as a trapper.

A BEAUTIFUL FRIENDSHIP

The card arrived in the mailbox in December. It was from a woman in Colorado who a few years ago introduced me to my friend Andy, who has since become my frequent partner on slow journeys over the bumpy face of Alaska.

Standing there in the post office, I felt a little funny when I saw the grainy illustration on the card: Two men in dark suits and hats, strolling down a path together. They cast one shadow on the path, because the men are holding hands.

"Best of luck on your ski to Nome," Mari wrote on the card. "Andy will be strong when you are not, and you will be strong when he is not."

Along with a touch of homophobia, the card triggered a pang of indecision. Andy had invited me to ski 700 miles across

Alaska with him, but I was struggling with the idea. The worst-case scenario of such a trip—getting caught between villages in a ground blizzard on the Bering Sea coast—played over and over in my mind.

I tucked Mari's card into my backpack a few days later, when I traveled to the White Mountains north of Fairbanks. I needed a bit of solitude to hash this one out.

It was early December, a time at this latitude when sunlight doesn't touch the frozen muskeg floors of some northern valleys. The starting point for the ski was the Tolovana River valley, about 100 miles south of the Arctic Circle. With optimism, I had one month earlier rented a cabin 32 miles from the parking lot at the western end of the White Mountains National Recreation Area. All I needed was a warm snap—a day with temperatures above zero—and I could skate-ski into the cabin in a few hours.

One month later, with less optimism, I checked the thermometer at my house in Fairbanks. Twelve below and falling. Along with a fresh snow, the temperature said skate skis were not right for this trip. I slid my classic skis into the bed of my truck.

I set out alone, grinding my skis over fresh snow crystals at 20 below zero. My skis stopped dead as soon as my muscles stopped pushing. Zero glide. I could walk as fast as I was skiing.

The slowness frustrated me, but it had its rewards—at walking speed, I saw the soft imprint of a lynx's body in the fresh snow covering the trail, and the silhouettes of black spruce trees leaned like crooked old men into the morning glow.

The work of moving forward kept me warm through the frigid air, which was trapped in the valley by a layer of warmer air above. Meteorologists call the phenomenon an inversion;

the valleys of interior Alaska have some of the strongest inversions on the planet.

I made it to a cabin 12 miles from the truck and called it good. Twelve miles had taken me five hours. There was no way I'd make it to the cabin I had rented 32 miles in. I didn't have enough food for that many hours on the trail, and, with the weather service predicting a drop to 30 below, skiing that far without a partner would be stupid. More important, skiing long distances at 30 below is not fun. The cold gnaws at places far from the heart; fingers and toes feel the sting first, then they go numb, forcing you to crank up the tempo. If the extra activity is not enough, thin layers of cells at the tips of fingers and toes freeze. I don't have a good time when I'm fretting about dead flesh.

Which is why, when I skied back to the truck the next day and saw a nearby outhouse thermometer at 39 below (how the hell am I going to start the truck?), I decided to tell Andy that I was not interested in a ski along the Serum Run trail, a 700-mile path on frozen rivers and overland between Nenana and Nome. As the cold nipped my fingertips while I changed into dry socks, I thought of facing this numbness day after day. I thought about windstorms on the Bering Sea coast that could "flash-freeze" you, as a Denali climbing ranger once described the fate of Japanese climbers exposed during winter on the mountain. I thought about skiing with a heavy backpack for one month. No thanks, Andy. Decision made.

After a failed attempt to warm my truck with a camping stove and five feet of stovepipe pointed at my oil pan, I walked to the Elliot Highway and flagged down a musher who was headed to Manley Hot Springs. She pulled out her jumper cables, and we got the Nissan started. I waited for the truck to warm up, and then began my two-hour drive back to Fairbanks. My radio picked up no signals along the Elliott Highway, and my cassette player was broken. I had no distractions from mulling the choice I'd just made not to do the trip with Andy.

I thought about the card in my backpack, the one that made me feel a bit strange when I saw the two men holding hands. Why would Mari send me something like that?

"You complement each other well on the crazy and scary things you do that make you know you're alive," she wrote.

Yeah. There was the time Andy insisted on carrying all our food when he joined me on a summer-long hike of the pipeline. Or when he calmly talked me out of charging up the wrong frozen creek during a 150-mile winter race because the tracks of another skier led that way. Or how sad he was when my dog died, and how he helped me dig her grave and then dragged me out on hikes afterward.

And I thought about spring, and how different Alaska was with three times the sunlight of that day's four hours: the smell of earth percolating through the snow, early-morning light that stirs the body and soul, and the songs of male chickadees, their tiny bodies flowing with testosterone in the spring sunshine. My brain, frozen in December's darkness, began to thaw.

A few months later, bags of Chex mix and animal crackers spilled from the top of two shopping carts as Andy and I walked down the aisles of Sam's Club in Fairbanks. The rolling pack train of junk food was to keep us sliding over the snow for the next month, as we skied the Serum Run trail, from Nenana to Nome.

We made the journey in 27 days. On one sun-drenched day in the middle of the trip, we covered 45 miles on snowmachine trail to reach the village of Tanana. It was a rare trail day when skate-skiing with a pack felt like dancing— effortless, rhythmic and fun. In the middle of that day, I looked ahead at Andy gliding through the trees. Tears he never saw came to my eyes when I thought of a line from Mari's card.

"Friends as good as you two are beautiful."

TEN YEARS AFTER

Ten years ago today, with two friends and a dog, I touched a chain-link fence in Valdez and started walking away from a sign that read "800," the mileage from there to Prudhoe Bay. I didn't stop for 120 days, at which time I had run out of summer and out of tundra, having reached a sign that read "0," and the Arctic Ocean.

Today is the anniversary of the first steps of a trip that will always define me as That Guy Who Hiked the Pipeline. With the perspective of a little time, I can now see how a summer-long walk along a road that parallels the trans-Alaska pipeline wouldn't appeal to most people. But I was smitten with the idea of being outside from the time buds on tree branches unfolded into leaves to the time those leaves turned yellow and fell to the ground. The trip still stands out as my favorite, and probably always will.

On that first day of hiking, May 4th, 1997, I was excited as a little boy on Christmas morning, not feeling the weight of that 70-pound pack in the cool, salty air of Valdez. I was starting a slow journey across Alaska, and walking with my dog and camping was the only thing on my calendar for the next four months.

I just walked, and watched my dog romp through the bushes, and stopped to filter water at streams that intersected my path so I could drink it. When I sat to pump water, I'd unlace my hiking boots to cool my feet in the breeze. That entire summer, I followed the rhythm of the trail, waking when the sun baked me from the tent and not shutting 'er down until midnight. I slept on carpets of reindeer moss, lichen, and smooth gravel, with a different bed each night.

With the summer sun always circling in the sky, the clock became irrelevant. No radio, no TV, no Ipod, nothing but bird songs, the wind through the trees, mosquito hum, the sounds of my hiking boots and the jingle of my dog's bear bell on her little pack. It was a good way to live.

Along the way, I met many more people than I imagined. I wrote newspaper columns for the Fairbanks paper every Sunday, and the editors included a front-page map that said "Keep Track of Ned & Jane." Some people sought us out. Delta Junction was the height of our celebrity, when during a two-day stretch more than a dozen different people took photos of Jane and I along the trail. Total strangers gave me smoked salmon, dog treats, Dr. Peppers, Sunday papers, white gas, fresh cucumbers, a little tape recorder, cool drinking water, a sling for my shotgun, and other useful items. I'm kind of a shy guy, but I enjoyed the attention. It was a summer that did a lot to solidify my idea that most people in this world have good hearts, and everybody has a good story.

Now, on this anniversary of the start of the hike, I page through my tiny journals from the trip. Here's a favorite night, as I was hiking with my friend John Arntz on the section of pipeline that parallels the Dalton Highway through the foothills of the Brooks Range.

Night 84, Pipeline Mile 284 (516 miles from Valdez). On a molar of rock above the Arctic Circle, from which I have perhaps the best view of the trip—360 degrees of green mountains, some treed, some domes of rock. John and I ate dinner on this rock, perhaps sitting where humans sat 1,000 years ago. Mosquitoes joust the wind in their quest for warm me. Two have tired; they now sit on my notebook ...

John and Jane, exploring after dinner, now stand on the next tor to the north, about one-quarter mile away and 50 feet lower than the jousting skeeters and me. The clouds to the northwest are the color of Rampart smoked salmon, the ridge in front as sharp as if cut by a razor.

It is a dream here. My dream. It has come true.

Sometimes, in the decade since the hike, I haven't dreamed as much, or I think other people will do it for me, which doesn't seem to happen. But that year, with that deliberate action, I nailed the way I wanted to live.

Ten years after, parts of that experience live on. John Arntz, who hiked 200 of the 800 miles with me, is still a good friend. He lives in San Francisco now, but we write almost every day. Our friendship was set in concrete on that trip, as was another, with my pal Andy Sterns. Others eroded away, as they will do when you don't work at them.

Almost everything else has changed since the hike along the pipeline: My dog Jane died three years after the walk, at the age of 13. My dad died a few months later. My mom died five years after my dad. I don't live in a one-room cabin anymore. I got married to a woman whose story spooked me for a few nights on the pipeline when I heard about this brown bear that attacked a biologist near Chitina. Two new dogs are in our lives, we have a baby, and we bought a house. Whew.

Sometimes I crave the simplicity I had during the summer of '97. To be outside during most of the hours of the summer is something I'd like to do every year. Walking everyday with no idea what your view will be during dinner makes for a pleasant, low-risk adventure. Covering miles at a leisurely pace, with an average of six to cover each day, adds to the enjoyment factor. I didn't feel like I was missing much ten summers ago. I was seeing the world around me, and there's not much that is more satisfying or nourishing.

I do miss that brown dog. Ten years ago, I wrote: *I hope this is Jane's best summer ever. There surely won't be another like it for her, or for me. Someday, in perhaps 10 or 20 years, I'll look back at photos from this trip and remember Jane, who will by then be in Doggy Heaven. I'll think of a wonderful summer in which a good dog got to be with her master 24 hours a day. And, lucky me, I got to be with her.*

Amen to that.

But even after dogs and people disappear from your life, there is renewal. On a whole new adventure, one that requires more than just physical endurance, I will carry a weight on my shoulders and in my arms every day this summer. She goes about 20 pounds, has the initials A.K., squints when she smiles, and laughs when you woof like a dog for her. Lucky me.

THE DOG AFTER

We lifted off from McCarthy towards Skolai Pass, three-and-one-half souls on board. Along with the pilot and my future wife Kristen was a black ball of fur, curled at Kristen's feet. The trip to the Goat Trail in Wrangell-St. Elias National Park was Chloe's first. The puppy was not yet six months old, and I wondered how she would handle the wild, gray-green world beneath us.

Chloe had a tough act to follow. I was still aching with memories of Jane, my chocolate Labrador retriever, who had died two months before. Jane had shared my 13 years in Alaska, and I was closer to her than to most people. She was my friend, a warm body that pressed against my sleeping bag at night, a travel partner, and part of my identity. When my father etched the names of my brothers, sisters, and their partners into a cement slab at the entrance to our childhood home years ago, he wrote "Ned and Jane."

I wasn't sure what to make of Chloe. She was Kristen's dog, even though I was along when Kristen picked her up from a woman in the Goldstream Valley for $30. People asked what breed Chloe was, and we shrugged: Border collie mom, dad with a good vertical leap enabling him to clear a fence. Jane was a purebred Lab, a beautiful creature with kind brown eyes, expressive brows and a groan when she plopped down that made her seem almost human.

Chloe is built like a creature of the desert—serpentine tail, snout like a fox, tubular body, spindly legs. Her ears belong on a mule deer. With them, she heard the laughter of a woman who passed us on a trail near home one day:

"That dog looks like a fruit bat."

Jane had met the fruit bat, and Jane wasn't thrilled. She was 13 then, in her last months of life, and here was a bouncing little pest that clamped onto the loose fur under her neck and tried to herd her. A few times, I had to cup my hands around the puppy's hips and pull her toward me when Jane was about to snap.

The contrast between them made my heart heavy. Chloe, lithe and flexible, showed that Jane was indeed an old dog, stiff and shaky, nearing the end. One of the saddest moments of my life was the time I closed the tailgate with my old friend in the back of the truck, getting ready to run the Angel Rocks trail with the new puppy. The trail was too steep for Jane, who had arthritis in her back. She looked at me from the back of the truck with sad brown eyes, as if she was letting me down.

When Jane died, I wrapped her in the chamois sheet that covered her couch and buried her at our favorite walking spot behind my cabin. At the grave, along with Kristen, friends Andy and Lisa and Lisa's dog Suzy, was Chloe. She had no sense of the gravity of the moment, and at one point dashed to the grave and mouthed the wild rose pedals Lisa had set there, shaking them to confetti.

Then, Chloe was all there was. She saved me from the empty dog-dish syndrome after Jane's death, but she was no Jane.

I had made it my mission to give Jane a happy life. I'd go bird hunting at 5 a.m. just to experience the teamwork of crawling to a pond together. I walked across Alaska with her when she was 10 years old, in large part because I wanted one summer when we could be together 24 hours a day.

With the loss of Jane came a waterfall of other changes, including the death of my father and a decision to move in with Kristen after living in a one-room cabin with Jane for more than a decade. I tried to push away as much of the change as possible, including the little black dog that used to ambush Jane.

But Chloe chipped away at my walls by expressing her own quirky personality. She was so excited in Skolai Pass that she nipped my pant legs, gently pinching my calves as she knew a good day in the outdoors was ahead.

Kristen, Chloe and I hiked up the broad saddle of Chitistone Pass, with Castle Mountain looming in the background and the ocean of Russell Glacier ice a few miles east. At its steepest, the Goat Trail is a narrow walkway of rock pressed into canyon walls by the footfalls of sheep, Native traders, and, after lonely men spread the word about gold in the town of Chisana in 1913, prospectors and pack horses who wanted to avoid a dreadful trip up the Nizina Glacier and Skolai Creek.

Many national parks, including Denali, don't allow dogs in the backcountry, but Wrangell St. Elias does, and I was glad of it. The more adventures I had with Jane, the more I trusted her not to run off after a moose calf or gallop back to me with a bear following. Now it was Chloe's turn to earn some trust. As a tiny pup, she had ridden in a fanny pack to a cabin in the White Mountains north of Fairbanks, but the days of the free ride were over; it was time to use her own skinny legs.

Two things stick in my mind when I remember the Goat Trail trip: River crossings and a wolverine. The river crossings scared me more than anything else. Jane would have dogpaddled across them, but Chloe was too small to cross the glacial creeks and the Chitistone River. I carried her in my arms across the smaller creeks, but when we came to the upper Chitistone I needed my arms free.

Kristen had an idea. She would ferry the pup across in her backpack, if we could get Chloe inside.

I hoisted Chloe and Kristen folded her legs into the backpack. We snugged the cord around Chloe's neck, securing all 30 pounds of her in a doggie straightjacket. Kristen and I each clamped onto a spruce pole with both hands, and I led us into the river. Invisible rocks detached beneath our boots and tumbled downstream. Cold water knifed through the seams of our rain pants and penetrated our boots. As our feet went numb, Chloe was silent, taking in the scene above Kristen's shoulders like a calm little Batman.

When we neared the end of the trip the next day, Chloe minded my heel command as we busted through an alder-choked trail next to the Chitistone. When we popped out of the brush and onto a gravel bar, Kristen squinted at something up ahead.

"Is that a bear cub?"

The wolverine shot a glance our way. We had caught it out in the open, at the river's edge. The wolverine wheeled around and tore back for the brush, kicking up a roostertail of sand.

Rather than chasing her first wolverine, Chloe stayed at our heels, tracking it with her radar ears and sniffing the air. The wolverine disappeared and Chloe looked up at me, waiting for the OK to start moving.

Chloe is now a regular companion on trips through Alaska. She makes me laugh as she throws a stick into the air and catches it after a long day, and she impresses me as she carries her doggie pack without whining. Chloe will never replace Jane, but she pads a bit deeper into my heart with every mile we cover.

THE LONGEST NIGHT

"We gained 18 seconds of light today," Dave said as he pulled his mountain bike from his car, its tires bouncing off snow as hard as concrete.

"Cool," somebody said.

Five of us were in the parking lot outside Ivory Jack's bar on December 22nd. We had gathered in the Goldstream Valley north of Fairbanks for the Longest Night Ride, put on by the Fairbanks Cycle Club. Our meeting time was 8 p.m., long after sunset, which wasn't hard to do on a day when the sun disappeared at 2:41 p.m.

We were one day past winter solstice, the shortest day of the year in the Northern Hemisphere, a day when there's enough cold and dark in Interior Alaska to make a person feel he's way too far north. It's the time of year when everyone Outside thinks we're nuts to live here. It's the time of year they're right.

To keep from going psycho when it's too cold for good camping and there's too little light for a ski trip, I celebrate the low point every year, sometimes just by lighting a candle. Other years I've hauled pallets to a windblown hillside above town, lit a solstice bonfire, stared into white heat and wondered what I was doing in this land of low light.

On the Longest Night Ride, we would pedal through the darkness on a network of local snowmachine trails also used by mushers, skijorers, runners, skiers and dog-walkers. The four other riders—Dave, Tom, Heike, and Malcolm—were diehard winter bikers equipped with featherweight bikes and doublewide Snowcat tires. I pulled from the garage my weighty steel Schwinn, purchased in 1989 with money earned by scrubbing Exxon Valdez-stained rocks.

Tom led us away from the artificial lights of Ivory Jack's and into a gap between leafless alders. We hit a feature that, to me, makes midwinter in Alaska bearable—a four-foot wide path of packed, dry snow that transformed summer's wet, unwalkable tundra into a smooth trail system that's more comprehensive than Alaska's highways. From our starting point at Ivory Jacks, we could splinter off to Nome, Anchorage, or, if we were really gluttons for the dark underbelly of winter, the North Slope.

We aimed a bit lower, agreeing on a 20-mile ride that looped through the Goldstream Valley and promised a return to Ivory Jack's before midnight.

I followed the blinking red light on the back of Malcolm's bike. Though I hadn't seen him much since then, I spoke to Malcolm every day in the fall of 1986, when he was my college roommate. Since then, he had become a disciple of winter biking, part of a cult of foam-bootied lean bodies who take to the trails with insulated handlebar pogies, tires that float upon punchy snow, and a giddiness when the forecast calls for cold weather that firms mashed-potato trails into white pavement.

Malcolm's taillight had a hypnotic effect as I stared at it while rolling over bumps on my smallest gear ring. I was grooving on how easy snow-riding was until we turned onto a less popular trail. There, my skinny tires cut deep grooves into the snow, I weaved to stay upright, and Malcolm's taillight shrunk to a pinpoint in the distance. He must have been looking back, because soon his headlight was blinding me.

"Try letting some air out of your tires," he said.

I deflated my tires to the point where my rims almost touched the snow. I hopped back on and peddled like mad to get on step.

When we caught up with the group, Tom looked at my skinny tires.

"Ned, why don't you lead the way? You'll get a firmer track by going first."

I led through dense willows, the light mounted on my handlebars framing the branches as if I was riding through a tunnel. Soon, my lighting system, a relic of the 80s, began to throw off a weak brownish beam, an indicator that my world would soon go dark.

My headlight died seconds later. Lit from behind by the bobbing headlights of the other riders, I veered off the trail into soft snow, my front tire pointing east on a trail going south. Tom laughed.

"You can go that way if you want," he said as he passed.

Letting the others ride on, I found it easier to see from behind them. Though the sun was overhead in New Zealand, it wasn't really dark on top of the world. The clouds that blanketed the Goldstream Valley reflected the city lights of Fairbanks over a ridge and onto the trail system.

I cranked along, my eyes gathering the faint light in a familiar way. From November to February, I spend a lot of time in the dark. I ski home from work at the university almost every night without a headlamp, but the night you encounter here isn't the tar-black of a midwinter night along a Nevada highway. The snowcover gives life to the little photons that bounce into our retinas, giving definition to trail bumps and tree branches.

And our short days aren't as brief as they seem. The sun rises at 11 and sets before 3 on the winter solstice in Fairbanks, but those numbers don't include our extra-long dawns and dusks. Those shoulder periods, called civil twilight, are light enough to allow you to tell a spruce tree from a birch tree. On winter solstice in Fairbanks, though the sun doesn't pop over the Alaska Range until 11, it's bright enough to travel outside at 9:30, and that same phenomenon lengthens the afternoons from 2:40 until 4, when the sky takes on the appearance of a pink and blue layer cake. Compare those three extra hours to the one hour per day of civil twilight San Francisco gets on solstice (just don't compare the air temperatures).

On the longest night ride, civil twilight was long gone when I saw the other bikers' blinking red taillights stacked on the side of the trail. I turned off into deep snow and heard the reason the others had pulled off—the puffs of breath from a team of 12 dogs. The musher behind them was running without a headlamp but clicked it on when he saw us.

"They're probably not used to seeing bikers out here this late," Tom said.

With the smell of dogs in the air, we started our return loop on the trail at 10 p.m. The longest night was about to give way to a slightly shorter one, and we had to work tomorrow.

The trail seemed to firm up a bit after our first pass, and I was seeing what those biking geeks liked about winter riding: the challenge of keeping the wheels moving fast enough so you don't bog down, the feeling of floating on air when you feel the trail more than you see it, and the silence of rubber knobs rolling over packed ice crystals. I could become a convert to winter biking if I weren't so addicted to skiing, and if my bike didn't weigh 70 pounds.

We made it back to Ivory Jacks near 11 p.m. on the longest night of the year. Malcolm had already peeled off, riding back to his woodstove and a late dinner. I pulled the front tire off my bike, hefted it into my car, and turned to Tom.

"Thanks for putting on the ride."

"Thanks for coming," he said. "Happy solstice."

LIFE IN THE VALLEY OF DEATH

I woke in the tent feeling the grit of volcanic ash between my toes, and I thought of my father. I had dreamed of him during the night, as winds swept the Valley of Ten Thousand Smokes and forced glassy dust inside. I rolled over in my sleeping bag and remembered that this day would have been his and my mother's 40th wedding anniversary.

Unzipping the tent door, I saw what looked like a desert with no cacti. While hiking in on the spongy surface of volcanic rock and ash a few days before, I had marked the transition from landscape to moonscape in my little notebook: the surrender of the willows as we hiked onto the ash sheet, the petering out of bird songs, the disappearance of mosquitoes. My first impression was that the Valley of Ten Thousand Smokes was the deadest place I'd ever seen.

For a few summer days in 1912, a hurricane of glowing dust and gases hot enough to vaporize flesh and bone swept through this remote Alaska valley where the Aleutian Islands connect to the mainland. The planet's largest volcanic eruption in the 20th century turned 40 square miles of the world's finest bear habitat into instant badlands. Botanist Robert Griggs, an early explorer of the valley, wrote that if the eruption had happened in Manhattan, people in Chicago would have heard the explosions.

Natives in the coastal village of Katmai evacuated a few days before the eruption because they felt the mountains shaking. The eruption destroyed the village, and one foot of ash fell on Kodiak, 100 miles away, but no one died. When Krakatoa volcano in Indonesia ejected half as much ash and rock in 1883, 35,000 people died.

On a National Geographic expedition in 1916, Griggs named the Valley of Ten Thousand Smokes for the geysers of steam over which he and his men cooked bacon on frying pans extended from long wooden poles.

Today, you can no longer fry bacon over fissures on the valley floor. The eruption laid down a glowing sheet of ash and rock more than 500-feet thick on the valley floor, but it has cooled after 90 years. The area is still alive with volcanoes; a half-dozen in Katmai National Park still exhale the sulfurous breath of the Earth.

As I got up to join the others in our party for breakfast, my dad stayed on my mind. He had died in upstate New York ten months before, just two months after the death of my dog Jane, who trotted happily by my side for all my 13 years in Alaska.

The one-two punch of losing my dog and then my dad left me in a funk I couldn't shake. At my father's funeral, a priest said my two brothers, two sisters and I would face a loss of identity with my dad gone. I thought of the priest's words many times when faced with self-doubt in the months after.

During the early 1990s when I worked as a park ranger on the Yukon River, I learned that being out in the quiet bogs, rivers and mountains of Alaska often could make me happy. All that changed after the losses of Tony and Jane. Hiking the same hills and valleys where Jane's wagging tail and the rest of her huggable body had accompanied me did not make me happy. I was adrift, my toehold on life swept away. My simple formula was not working anymore.

The Valley of Ten Thousand Smokes was a new place for me, different from anywhere else I'd ever been. My guide was John Eichelberger, a 52-year-old volcano researcher who had invited me and 11 other people on his annual trip to the valley. Eichelberger has a sourdough's beard, a fondness for singing maritime songs from the 1800s and a wistful sense of adventure.

On one of our final days in the valley, John had planned for us yet another hike. In ten days of glorious sunshine, those of us who chose to follow John's lead up volcanoes and into remote corners of the valley walked more than 70 miles. That morning's hike was an attempt at Trident Volcano, a snow-covered 6,000-foot peak with a knife-edge ridge leading to the summit.

We set out walking across the ash and rock that coats the valley. The rock, so low in density it floats, was spewed from a volcanic vent that looks like a gray crumb cake and is the size of a domed stadium. Griggs named it Novarupta, Latin for "New Vent," and we walked past it to get closer to Trident Volcano, which last erupted from 1953 to 1960.

We hiked along a mushy snowfield to Katmai Pass, a saddle between volcanoes that Natives, explorers and bears have used for centuries to reach the Bering Sea or the Pacific Ocean. Along the way, we caught wisps of sulfur that made me hungry for a tuna fish sandwich. We then moved into a fog that hid the sun and caused water droplets to cling to the slightest peach fuzz on our faces.

I pulled my map and compass from my raincoat pocket and we followed the needle southeast through the pure white world of fog on snow. While I was squinting ahead for black volcanic rocks that were the only points of reference, a silhouette approached. As it came closer, we recognized the wolverine's weasel-like gallop. It stopped about 30 feet away and sniffed the air then wheeled away.

I looked around. Katmai Pass—filled with snow and fog and jagged black rock that had spilled from the vent of Trident Volcano—looked even less capable of supporting life than the rest of the valley. And here was a wolverine, a rugged scavenger that covers ultramarathon distances every day to find food and stays hidden even from biologists who spend months trying to see it.

The sight of the wolverine waddling into the mist gave me that feeling again. I felt I was in the right place, and I wouldn't trade places with anyone in the world. Any ground you share with these beasts is sacred ground. Wolverines will not tolerate our roads, the throb of our engines, the smell of burned heating oil. Where you find the wolverine, it seems you find the essence of Alaska.

In the days ahead, we noticed life all over the valley. Scrub willows anchored in pumice on slopes protected from the wind; ptarmigan huddled over eggs on shallow bowls of volcanic rock; and, on our final day, a mother grizzly followed her nose through the valley, towing a cub on a crooked path over the lunar landscape. John said the bear was the first he had seen in the valley in his 20 years of visiting there.

I left the Valley of Ten Thousand Smokes a somewhat different person than when I had entered. Wild Alaska had lifted me out of the hole I'd been in the past year, at least for the 10 days we were in the valley. My system was working again. Like the plants and creatures thriving in that beautifully barren place, I was alive.

WHITE RICE ON THE WEST BUTTRESS

"Don't go up Denali with the Japanese, Ned, they're not like you."

On an elevator ride at work a few years ago, a coworker gave me some advice when I told him about an opportunity I might have to join a team of Japanese climbers in repairing a weather station on Mt. McKinley.

"Those guys are built to survive the cold," he said. "They don't have long fingers and noses that freeze like yours and mine. They won't care about you up there."

His words, delivered with conviction, bugged me, but I didn't think of them again until one summer when I landed on the southeast fork of the Kahiltna Glacier with six climbers straight from Tokyo and two men of Japanese descent from Fairbanks. One of those Alaskans, Tohru Saito of the International Arctic Research Center, had recruited me on a month-long mission with a Japanese climbing team to repair a weather station perched at 19,000 feet on North America's highest peak.

I felt like I'd hit the lottery. I've spent many winter moments looking southwest from Fairbanks at the distant molar that is Denali. More than once I've wanted to stand on top of that magnificent lump, and here was a chance.

There were a few complications. Number one, I had zero mountaineering experience. Number two, I spoke no Japanese. Tohru, fluent in both languages, assured me that I would do fine so long as I followed the directions of trip leader Yoshi-tomi Okura, a mountaineer famous in Japan for his winter climbs in the Himalayas and 13 consecutive summits of Mt. McKinley. I might also want to bring some Western food to supplement my diet, Tohru said.

"You're going to eat a lot of rice."

Our first meal at the Kahiltna base camp at 7,300 feet was rice, smothered in soy sauce with meat chunks. We ate in a group of nine sitting next to one another, which was to be our custom on the mountain.

Of the six climbers from Japan, one spoke a bit of English, and he was happy to practice it on me. Takeshi Ogawa was 60 years old, the eldest member of our climbing team. He was upbeat about everything, including the snow that fell in his bowl while we ate some meals standing up. Thirty years ago, on his last trip to Alaska, he had climbed two nearby mountains—Mt. Foraker and Mt. Hunter. Lacking the money to fly out, he and his climbing partners had walked back to Talkeetna, 50 miles away.

Ogawa-san, as everyone called him, always popped from his tent with a broad smile. "It's a perfect day," were his first words, even on zero-degree mornings. He had retired as an architect, he told me, and he was now getting back into mountaineering. He showed me pictures of his daughter, and his beautiful wife, who a few years ago had "gone to Heaven." He seemed to be one of those people who lives his life as if every day is precious. I stayed close to him.

I shared a tent with Tohru and Yoshi, who had both grown up in Alaska. Besides Ogawa-san, the Japanese in our party included Maki and Jun, two lanky guys in their 20s who prepared most of the food for us. Other Japanese were journalist Hiroshi Morita, real-estate agent Makoto Somiya, and our leader, Yoshitomi Okura.

Okura, 52, was the undisputed boss, and the others would go silent around our snowy dinner platform when he spoke of the next day's plans, which Tohru would translate for me.

Okura was the type of bulldog mountaineer my coworker warned me about in the elevator years before. He was shorter than me but more solid, and the way he combed his black hair made him look like '70s tough guy Charles Bronson. His skin was tanned the color of a rare steak, and, unlike the rest of us, he didn't break out his down jacket at the lower camps on the mountain, shivering in his pile pullover to get acclimated to the cold.

Okura always poured green tea for each of us in turn before filling his own cup. When he smoked cigarettes, which he did only at the lower camps, he would flick his ash not on the snow, but in the blue garbage bag that National Park Service rangers give to climbers.

I trusted Okura with every decision, which was a strange sensation for me; I'm usually in control of everything on trips, from food to route choice, but I was happy to follow Okura on the beaten snow path up Denali's West Buttress route.

And I never got tired of rice. With the young studs Jun and Maki carrying such weighty items as a two-liter bottle of soy sauce, dinner was always tastier than the freeze-dried dinners I would have brought. We ate food I didn't know existed, including the canned liver of a lantern fish, the minced brain of king crab, 100-year-old fermented eggs, spiced plums, and my favorite, smoked eel over rice.

After 17 days we had climbed to "high camp," and made our home behind a wall of snow blocks at about 17,000 feet. The next morning, Jun, Maki and Okura carried the weather station equipment to our objective, a titanium stand wired to rocks above Denali Pass. Okura had installed the stand there in 1990 because he believes it is the location where three of his friends were blown off the mountain and killed during a winter climb. Ever since, he has had a passion for recording the wind speed and temperature at the site. Because winter winds can top 100 miles per hour at the station, it breaks often.

We spent one-and-one-half hours above most of the world's oxygen molecules at the station, removing and replacing weather instruments and tying off cables. When we finished and took some photos, it was time to head for the summit.

I knew something was wrong with me as soon as I resumed climbing. I felt like I was sleepwalking behind Jun, as if I couldn't keep my eyes open. He patiently waited when he felt the rope jerk behind him, and we stopped for a break. I thought a snack might clear my head, so I tore open a bag of Japanese crackers.

I soon found myself on all fours, emptying the contents of my stomach onto the snow 1,000 vertical feet and one horizontal mile from the top of North America. As I retched, I felt the hand of Jun, patting the back of my down jacket.

"Neddo is OK?"

I retreated to high camp with Tohru, who had also had trouble with the altitude. As we passed Okura, he nodded from the back of the rope, agreeing that descending was the right thing to do.

The next morning, I was bummed for failing to reach the summit, but I was the only one to whom it mattered. The Japanese, who had all made it to the top, were their usual cheerful selves, and Okura later toasted our success with a shared Miller Lite, saying that having everyone safe and healthy was the real victory.

After 21 days on the mountain, we descended into the thicker air of the lowlands on a crystal clear day, skiing down the Kahiltna Glacier toward the 7,300-foot base camp. Here was the only place I was stronger than the Japanese, because many had never skied before.

My friend Ogawa-san tumbled to the snow again and again, with his heavy sled jackknifing behind him. When he finally made it down the last hill, he fell again, then got up laughing.

"What a beautiful skier I am," he said.

Thinking back to that moment, I realize that the guy in the elevator was right—the Japanese are not like me. They're a lot more fun to travel with.

GOING IT ALONE

My friends aren't going to make it today. It's about 10 p.m. here on a frozen river way up north, and I don't hear the sound of voices carrying across the valley.

It's a bit lonely up here, camping on the snow at a time when most of the state is brown and green. I've been on the North Slope caribou hunting on skis for three days, and tonight I was hoping to see friends who had planned to drive up the Dalton Highway, walk in six miles on snowshoes, and join me at a spot I'd marked on their map. But they are not here.

This extreme quiet, so silent that the landscape hums, is a gift, but it's one that is better shared. I haven't spoken to anyone for three days, and I've got nothing left to tell myself.

Being alone was good for the caribou hunting, though. I stalked a few animals on skis last night, had a favorable breeze, and a nice clump of frozen tundra upon which to prop my elbows. I shot a small bull that died quickly. Within two hours, I had him field-dressed in an icy wind that froze his liver where I placed it on the snow.

The last big animal I shot was a moose, one decade ago. Though I've tried very hard to duplicate that hunt, the meat in game bags nearby is the first I've harvested in a long time.

Wearing white pants and a white anorak my friend BJ loaned me, I stalked the caribou the way I wanted, without worrying if another person's motion or scent would give up our position. By myself, I made all the decisions: when to stop skiing and walk on the wind-packed snow; where to start curving around the white dome; when to start belly-crawling to the clump of tundra.

The kill and the field dressing were matter-of-fact: no one to high-five, no one to hold legs while I started skinning. I gave a big Thank You to the sky above and started in, being extra careful not to cut myself with the knife. A self-inflicted wound seemed like one of the biggest risks of going it alone.

I enjoyed the skinning and quartering of the animal because I like that sort of stuff and because the caribou's heat kept my hands warm. I felt good when I separated each large hunk of meat and set it out on clean snow to cool. I felt even better when I returned to camp that night with the animal in my sled.

Now, drinking my last cup of tea before crawling into the tent, I think of how nice it would be for my friends to see that heavy sled, and to share this pot of tea with someone. But it's just me in this narrow river valley, pointy black mountains climbing from each side of the groove created by the river.

The frost forming on my neck gaitor tells me it's going to be another cold night. The meat in the sled is already hard as stone.

I brush my teeth and pause, straining to hear voices in the white light of 11 p.m., but nothing stirs. Then I crawl into the tent, page through an old Western, and fall asleep.

In the morning, I linger in the sleeping bag because the air has dropped below zero, which I knew during the night when I shivered myself awake a few times. I pop out of the tent when I hear a snippet of human voice over the wind. I stand up on my packed snow platform and hear it again; it's the voice of my friend Chris, I think.

I yell, hear nothing, and then squint around the dazzling white valley. Looking through binoculars, I see two stick figures about two miles off on a hillside. I yell again, wave, think I see the figures stop, and then watch them stalk a few caribou while I gather snow for morning coffee. I yell a few more times, but they melt over a ridge and out of my viewshed.

Hmmm. I had planned on skiing out this morning, but I looked forward to a night of camping with my friends. But maybe those two were someone else. If I knew them, they would have waved back, right?

With my friends no longer in sight and with what waits for me—a seven-mile ski, the cold start of a Subaru that hates cold starts, and 400 miles of driving—I decide to ski out.

After a short climb to a ridge to see if perhaps my friends had a base camp close to me, I ski back down to pack up my sled. On top of the frozen bags of meat, I set my rifle, then cover everything with a tarp and tie it with parachute cord.

On my ski out on the river, I look back at the hillside where the stick figures had disappeared. Nothing.

Ravens grab my attention. A dozen yelling, swooping black birds give life to the white landscape.

"Gut pile," I think. "Some hunter got a caribou nearby."

There are a few problems with that theory; I had seen no other people on my ski from the road a few days before, and I am now three miles from the highway, well within the no-hunting corridor.

Looking to where the ravens congregate on a south-facing slope, I see an answer I didn't expect. Rumbling down the hillside is a familiar but out-of-place mass of brown: A grizzly bear.

I hadn't thought about bears the night before, when I slept next to my sled full of meat. In late April, it is still below zero at night; how could bears be out of hibernation?

Logic doesn't matter. This bear is out, he looks fat and sassy, and he is now galloping down the hill toward me.

There aren't many times in life when you feel like prey. My experience goes like this: I see the bear, know he sees me, realize he probably has a carcass to protect, remember my gun is tied in a sled behind me. To reach it, I'll need to drop my backpack, ski back to the sled, untie a slipknot, grab the gun, bolt a shell into the chamber, and remain calm.

No time for that. With ski poles in hand, I raise them over my head and hit the aluminum shafts together, hoping the tic-tic-tic will be foreign enough to stop the bear.

I can almost see the sound waves hitting the bear. He stops in mid-gallop, half-stands, and turns back up the hillside. I exhale.

Twitching with adrenaline, I horse my sled up the opposite hill to a point where I feel safe enough to rub climbing skins onto my ski bases. With that task done, I pull out the binoculars and watch the bear from across the valley. Protecting its unidentified carcass, it nips at ravens that dance just out of reach.

I pause every few minutes to watch the bear in the hours it takes me to haul the sled uphill, feeling lucky to have squeaked through the encounter. With someone else along, I would have felt an illusion of security, thinking a bear would be less likely to approach a group of people. But it was just me, a grizzly bear, and a sled full of meat. Now, on the other side, I know I've had one of those moments that will stick in my mind for a long time. And I'm glad I had the chance to face it alone.

FINDING FAULT

A Greek philosopher once claimed that a person could not step into the same river twice. His words might also apply to rivers of ice.

Thirteen years had passed since I last stepped on Canwell Glacier. Back then, I had skied onto the Alaska Range glacier with three friends and two dogs. The dogs are now running together in Doggy Heaven, and my three travel companions and I have never followed up on our plans to do more trips together.

The Canwell Glacier has also slimmed down a bit since the spring of '89. U.S. Scientists have measured nearby Gulkana Glacier for decades, and have found that, in the last 13 years, it has lost about 175 cubic kilometers of water. Though no one has the numbers, its neighbor the Canwell has probably shrunk in a similar fashion. Except for the sharp outlines of white mountains to the south, everything here feels different than it did in 1989.

For one thing, it's raining. The mist on the tent fly reminds me of late August, but we are here in late November. A Chinook wind from Hawaii is curling over the mountains and spilling warm air over the glacier, whipping the flaps of my friend Adam's tent. In 1989, Adam was a freshman at Ladysmith High School in rural Wisconsin. He has since migrated north, gotten married, and earned a master's degree in the study of glaciers.

Today we have both walked onto the Canwell, Alaska's most mispronounced glacier. Many people can't resist inserting a "t," but Cantwell Glacier and the town of Cantwell are on the other side of the Alaska Range. Explorer E.F. Glenn named this glacier after Private Canwell of his hospital corps in 1898.

On this evening, 104 years after Glenn passed by, the tent amplifies the November rain, but the drops are as gentle as they are freakish. Adam and I crawl out for one last look around. We walk to the top of a mound of gravel and see something odd: a glow emitting from near the Delta River. Contractors have set up lights so they can work through the darkness in an attempt to re-center the trans-Alaska pipeline on its supports. A few weeks ago, the largest earthquake on the planet in 2002 released a good deal of its energy here. Workers are now scrambling to make things right.

Adam and I are camping on the Denali fault, which has created and maintained the trench in which the Canwell Glacier lies. We have traveled here because we want to see what the earthquake has wrought, before snowfall, spring melt, and the glacier's flow soften its effects.

As far as earthquakes go, the Denali fault earthquake was a cranker. When viewed from a small plane, the scar of the Denali fault earthquake looks as if a farmer dragged a giant plow across Alaska, ripping a 200-mile furrow through tundra, rock, and ice.

One of the greatest wonders of the magnitude 7.9 earthquake was that no one died during or after its shaking. A similar earthquake in 1906 destroyed San Francisco and killed more than 700 Californians.

The Denali fault earthquake released its energy in a swath that intersected no major cities, but it throttled Mentasta Pass, Tok, Northway, and Beaver Creek in the Yukon. The earthquake sheared the Richardson Highway and Tok Cutoff Road, rattled cans from shelves, and snapped water and fuel lines, but the earthquake was remarkably gentle to our species. The earthquake's ferocity is best seen in its effects on the glaciers that creep over it.

Our night on the Canwell Glacier is so warm that I pull off my socks in my sleeping bag. In the morning, the Chinook is still with us; I strip off my gloves to eat breakfast. Only the low angle of the sun, which will not top the wall of mountains to the south, reminds us it is winter.

After breakfast, we cache most of our stuff under rocks, Adam marks our pile's location on his GPS, and we start hiking up the glacier to see how the Canwell has changed.

We soon find a blue basin filled with jigsaw pieces of ice.

"This used to be a lake," Adam says. "The earthquake probably drained it in a hurry."

I hold up a triangle of ice and try to imagine the collapse of a glacial lake as big as a football field, and the pulse of water that bulged Miller Creek on its way to the Delta River.

We hike upglacier on boulders covered with melting snow. To the west, the Chinook wind stacks lenticular clouds over the mountains.

We stop at a fracture of clear ice that appears to have snapped shut on a falling rock, which is now suspended like a stick in a crocodile's mouth. We see cracks in the ice so straight they seem manmade. We pull off our gloves to touch smooth whale bellies of ice thrusting from the glacier.

As the light fades, we see what we are looking for—an immense crack, running up the north side of the glacier. We hustle over to the fault trace, the ruptured line that betrays the slashing movement along the Denali fault.

Adam follows the rip to a meltwater streambed worn into glacier ice. Half of the stream's channel has been moved 15 feet up the glacier, as if by a D-9 Cat. Adam explains the earthquake's textbook behavior:

"The Denali is a strike-slip fault with right-lateral motion," he says. "That means when you stand facing the fault trace, the land on the other side is moving to the right."

Over time, earthquakes along the Denali fault have moved mountains. Rocks on one side of the fault don't match their neighbors on the other side. A long time ago, the rocks that built Mt. McKinley lived near Tok; earthquakes over the years have ratcheted them a few hundred miles westward, in fits and starts.

We follow the crack down the glacier, pausing to take a photo where the earthquake shoved up two spikes of ice like five-foot rabbit ears.

As Adam stands between the ice ears, I try to imagine the drama of being on the glacier during that earthquake, with ice lunging into the air like some creature from the deep. And what did a rupture that tore across Alaska at three miles per second sound like?

While gawking at the rip in the glacier, we burn all our daylight. Adam and I switch on headlamps, and he hands me his GPS. I have never used one before. The last time I was on the glacier, I never dreamed that satellites could someday lead my back to my food bag. And though I slept for three nights on the glacier 13 years ago, I had no idea that the Canwell would someday be torn in half like a phone book, and I would never again step onto the little glacier I knew.

SNAG'S HEART OF COLD

One.

It's the reason Jim and I are here, camping on the white flat of a dead airstrip with no noise but our voices, and nothing for miles but the ghost town of an Indian village.

One is the difference in degrees Fahrenheit between Alaska's all-time low temperature and the North American record of 81 degrees below zero, set where we pitch the tent. Jim and I are daring the weather gods to give us their best shot by camping in the coldest place in North America in mid-January.

That place is Snag, Yukon Territory, which is today an abandoned airstrip being reclaimed by balsam poplars and haunted by the shells of buildings that shielded a small group of men from the coldest air ever recorded from Panama to Barrow.

Eighty-one below. I can't imagine it. The coldest temperature I've felt in Fairbanks was 56 below, during a cold snap in January 1989. I've been here for 20 winters now and have seen 50 below just once, during that week in January. Back then, I took a photo of a thermometer outside my cabin window before taking my dog on a short walk, during which she held up her paws every few steps as if she was walking on coals. I stuffed my wood stove with birch that night, but still saw my breath the next morning and found my dog's dish frozen to the floor.

I stopped driving during that cold spell after laughing with my friend Anna while counting seven broken fan belts on the streets of Fairbanks. We stopped laughing when hers became the eighth, and we had to zoom to an auto parts store before her engine, in cosmic irony, overheated because her fan stopped moving.

The cold affected lots of things. My cheap telephone got so cold inside the cabin that its ring weakened to the chirp of a cricket. Then it got colder and the ringer died, so I couldn't hear when my phone was ringing. This wasn't good for my mother's nerves. She, after seeing national news reports of the cold snap in Fairbanks, called and called with no answer. She then dialed the local chapter of the Red Cross and asked them to search for my frozen carcass. I sheepishly told the officer I was alive when he contacted me at the office of the university newspaper.

That was cold. But it was no 81 below, a number that fascinates me, and even more so Jim. He is a forecaster for the National Weather Service, and is a bit groggy after getting off the midnight shift. He has missed a night's sleep, but could not resist a midwinter's journey to Snag.

"When you've been up 24 hours, it's like you drank a six-pack," he said on our drive across the Alaska/Canada border to Beaver Creek, where we spent a night at Buckshot Betty's before heading out to Snag.

Jim and I are both a bit obsessed with the cold, which is probably why Fairbanks pulled us in. I remember being riveted to a TV broadcast of Jack London's "To Light a Fire" when I was a boy growing up in New York. A victim of hubris, London's character perished at 75 below. Even fiction can't top Snag.

With his beard at its bushiest, Jim looks as if he could be pushing a shopping cart on the streets of San Francisco. His beard now gathers frosts to the point where he's blending in with the snow-covered trees.

Jim's a good travel partner because he's got the fitness base to ski the 18 miles to Snag from the Alaska Highway without a whimper, and because he's fun to hang out with. He's the guy whose voice you hear above the crowd at running races and post-race bonfires. He laughs even louder than he talks, and--an added bonus for this trip--he's a savvy weatherman who can answer all my questions about the cold.

We are tenting on a plateau above the White River, the waterway that clouds the mighty Yukon with a load of silt from the Wrangell Mountains in Alaska and the St. Elias Mountains in Canada. Snag takes its name from the nearby Snag Creek, which explorers named after extricating their boats from driftwood snarls where the creek flows into the grand expanse of the White River.

This day is gray and 5 above zero, almost 100 degrees warmer than February 3, 1947, when a group of Canadians served their country in a few buildings that decompose nearby. On that day, four weathermen each made hushed pilgrimages to the alcohol thermometer near the airstrip with snow squeaking beneath their mukluks. At 7:20 a.m. one of them filed a notch onto the glass casing of the bulb to mark the lowest temperature he had ever seen. When they later sent the thermometer to Toronto, officials there confirmed the temperature at Snag had dropped to minus 81.4 degrees Fahrenheit (minus 63 Celsius).

Wilf Blezard was one of the men stationed at Snag that day. He's 82 now, and living in Grande Prairie, Alberta. He said Snag existed to make sure aircraft flying from Edmonton to Anchorage or Fairbanks had a place to land in case of trouble. Snag was his duty station for just seven months, from January to July 1947. As a 26-year-old World War II veteran, Blezard dropped into Snag at the same time a dome of fiercely cold air was settling in.

"We had six dogs that stayed outside the barracks," Blezard said over the phone from Grande Prairie. "Their breath created quite a fog above them . . .When a plane flew over at 10,000 feet, it sounded like it was in your bedroom."

The dogs are long gone, and so are the planes, as Jim and I eat freeze-dried dinners on an airstrip as silent as it once was cold. Looking around, something puzzles me about Snag. After a few minutes, it hits me—the coldest air I've felt in Alaska has pooled in low places, but the Snag airstrip sits on a bench above the White River, 1,925 feet above sea level.

"How can this be the coldest spot, when we're so high?" I ask.

"You've got to zoom out to the big picture," Jim says. "We're surrounded by big mountains (of the Wrangell-St.Elias ranges). We're in the drainage of all the cold air that forms up high, and the mountains block any warm, moist air that might come in from the Gulf of Alaska. And a lack of moisture makes for a lack of clouds, so there's nothing to trap the little heat that's here. It all drifts off into space."

It is impressive that this spot beat out the Old Crows, the Tananas, the Fort Yukons, and all the other frigid, low-lying places that have enough people to merit official thermometers.

"There probably were colder spots," Jim says, "but we don't have a lot of observing sites compared to the amount of area we have."

Alaska's coldest temperatures on Snag's big day in 1947 were minus 75 in Tanacross, 70 below in Northway, and 68 below in Fort Yukon the day after. Alaska came within a frosted eyelash of knocking Snag from the cellar on January 23, 1971. On that day, weather observers at Prospect Creek, a pipeline camp 25 miles southeast of Bettles, recorded Alaska's all-time low of 80 degrees below. The temperature at Snag that day was unavailable; the Canadian military had pulled out from the airstrip, alcohol thermometers and all, in 1967.

ESKIMO BASEBALL

As a rosy twilight hung over Norton Bay, Hal Needham and I walked the streets of Koyuk, a village of about 300 people on the Seward Peninsula. A September chill kept us moving with hands in pockets, until we heard the thud of an aluminum bat hitting a tennis ball.

Boys and girls were playing a game that looked like baseball, only there didn't seem to be any bases. The field was a gravel road, but the laughs, yells, and energy level reminded me of playing backyard ball every summer night in upstate New York when I was a boy. Standing in western Alaska as a 42-year-old, I wished I could join the Koyuk version of pickup baseball. Hal read my mind, and then nudged me with his elbow.

"Let's get out of our comfort zone," Hal said. "Let's ask these guys if we can play."

Hal approached the kids.

"Can we join you guys?" he asked.

"Sure," said a teenage Native boy, pointing at Hal. "You on our team and him on the other."

After shedding my coat, I stood in line behind a little guy named Ben, who looked like a miniature whaling captain. When his turn at-bat came, Ben touched the bat to a weathered tennis ball held up by a raven-haired girl, Luanne. Luanne then tossed the ball straight up and Ben smacked it as it came down. It bounced to an older boy, and Ben chose not to run to the safe zone at the other end of the road, as was his option in what the kids called "Eskimo baseball."

Hitting next, I dribbled a grounder on the street and sprinted to the other end, trying to dodge Albert's throw after he retrieved the ball from under a boat. When he nailed me in the back, the teams switched sides.

Some of the kids wore only t-shirts as the night air temperature dropped below freezing. They were silent with concentration at the plate and jawed at each other in the field. My heart thumped with adrenaline every time I came to bat, and when I ran I juked to avoid the thrown ball. It brought back memories of the old neighborhood; I could almost hear Mom calling me to dinner.

When the sun dropped behind the spruce hillside, the ball began to disappear into shadows when it left the bat, and the kids drifted home one by one. Hal and I pulled on our coats and walked back to a school building where we were spending the night.

Scuffing the gravel on the hike down to the school, I realized how lucky we just were. Alaska has a couple hundred

Native villages, many of them reachable only by boat or plane, and over the years I've skied or walked through a few. They always intrigue me, but I'm usually too bashful or gassed from the day's effort to look beneath the surface.

One time, in Nulato, when Andy Sterns and I were skiing the Serum Run trail, the body of a boy who committed suicide was at rest in the community center. The storekeeper said we were welcome to walk over and view the body, but we had skied many miles that day, and Andy and I stayed in the school library, ate a village-store pizza and fell asleep. I thought about that kid the whole next day when I was skiing down the Yukon.

The next night, in Kaltag, the locals held a "stick dance," to honor their recently departed relatives. That time, I pulled on my down booties and walked over to the community hall for the celebration. My father had died a few months before, and the stick dance was something I wanted to see, even if it cost me recovery time. That night, people from Kaltag and surrounding villages dressed in clothes that resembled those favored by the departed. Until the sun came up the next day, they sang ancient songs and danced around a tall spruce pole in the center of the community hall. I hung back in the shadows of the hall and watched.

Kaltag and other Native villages fascinate me because they are such a major part of what Alaska is, but most of them are so isolated a person could spend a lifetime in the state without visiting one. I'm a passing stranger in the villages, often traveling by unusual (and by many villagers' standards, slow and impractical) means. My friend Andy taught me to be unassuming while traveling through villages, and to keep in mind that while I might think my trip is a big deal, it is a mistake to assume that locals feel the same way.

The villages and the soft-spoken people who live there are mysteries to a white, urban-Alaska dweller like me; that's what made the game of Eskimo baseball such a rare treat. Hal and I chased that tennis ball, pegged it at each other and the kids, and felt like we were 10 years old. There were only a few moments of self-consciousness, like the time I glanced into the window of a plywood house and saw the dark eyes of a Native man looking back, wondering what to make of me and the smiling six-foot giant playing with his children.

The next morning, waiting for a plane to Nome, Hal and I saw the same group of village kids gathered outside the school on a basketball court made of treated two-by-sixes. Since they'd introduced us to Eskimo baseball, we asked the kids if they wanted to try Wiffle ball.

Traveling through Nome a week earlier, we saw at a local store the yellow bat with the ball attached to the handle, and I bought it at what I thought was the highest price in North America (until we went to a nearby hardware store and found a set for a dollar more). Wiffle bats and balls have ridden across Canada and the U.S. in the trunk of my car, and I have floated knucklers to my brother high in the Alaska Range. Hal and I thought the Wiffle set would come in handy while waiting out flights in Seward Peninsula villages on a trip to install weather stations at schools.

The Koyuk kids joined us in a game with the weightless bat and "the plastic ball that curves." We split into teams on the basketball court, and the kids lined up and waited their turn to bat. Some caught on to the rules of American baseball; some didn't remember to run every time they hit the ball or advance on the bases. Some kids, the natural athletes who would look graceful hauling a seal out of Norton Bay, smacked home runs over the chain-link fence.

Our Wiffleball clinic lasted for more than an hour when our plane buzzed over the town. Hal and I grabbed our packs and hopped onto the back of a four-wheeler for a ride to the airstrip.

When the airplane lifted off, we banked for Nome. Looking down over Koyuk, I saw the kids had left the basketball court and had reassembled back on the street for a game of Eskimo baseball. Their moving figures 500 feet below brought back the night before: under orange light on a hillside above the ocean where people had lived for centuries, we became part of the noise and the motion for a few hours, thanks to little people who weren't afraid to let strangers take a few cuts.

END OF THE ROAD

Riding the smooth, brown surface of the Yukon River, I dipped a paddle and aimed the canoe at Pickerel Slough, a crooked finger of blue that pointed north. The map showed a cabin there, and the mystery of it pulled me in.

Once on the flat water of the slough, I saw a log cabin, shrouded in weeds but livable. I tied the canoe to a log and walked up a sandy path.

I yelled hello, heard no reply, and pushed open the door. When my eyes adjusted to the darkness, there was no mistaking who had last slept there. Crutches leaned against a wall. Cardboard boxes addressed to Dennis Tucker were strewn about, and a letter he was drafting to a district attorney lie on the floor. On the log wall hung a page torn from a bible: *David kills Goliath.*

Dennis Tucker was not home. He was in a jail cell in Fairbanks; two weeks earlier he had fired 15 bullets into a Super Cub as it sat parked on an airstrip in the town of Eagle. I had heard the shots on that hot June day, and minutes afterward had watched Tucker's retreat on crutches to his campsite down on the river. A few hours later, troopers in flak jackets converged on the blue tarp that Tucker was living beneath and handcuffed him without a struggle. He was soon in a helicopter bound for Fairbanks, where he was charged with felony criminal mischief.

Even though I knew Tucker was not watching me from the woods, a chill ran from my toes to the top of my head as I stood inside the cabin. I stepped outside to the light for a few minutes and looked around at the splendor of Pickerel Slough.

Rising from the backdrop of the old river channel were gray limestone spires that jutted from a hillside like bad teeth. Not long after I had entered the slough, a bull moose exploded from the water, its antlers fuzzy with velvet and its coat shedding gallons of water as it stomped onto a bank. While the moose grunted through the brush, a mother grebe floated by, followed by nine tiny clones.

The slough was one of the prettiest places I had seen on the Yukon during my two years there as a park ranger. As I stood at the cabin door, I couldn't help but think that living in a place with all that silence was perhaps too much of a good thing for a person like Dennis Tucker.

I knew Tucker's story because I was a park ranger who wanted to be a writer, and the guy with the crazy hair and a furry beard was a story waiting to happen. He lived on a park bench overlooking the Yukon when I first saw him. He was dressed in camouflage fatigues, with a handgun on his hip and a rifle slung over his shoulder.

I interviewed some of the Eagle locals about Tucker, and I later interviewed Tucker when he was in jail. This was his story:

He had appeared in Eagle one summer wanting to live in the Bush. He mentioned John McPhee's *Coming into the Country* as one of the reasons he chose Eagle, a town of about 150 people at the end of the Taylor Highway. During the next 11 years, Tucker lived in and around Eagle, in canvas wall tents, under tarps or sometimes in deserted cabins. Like many who seek an independent lifestyle in the Bush, Tucker found that he couldn't do it alone. He needed an occasional boat ride down the Yukon River or maybe a place to sleep when he visited town. The people of Eagle helped him, and that's where the story turned.

While staying in a wall tent outside Eagle one winter, for reasons not even he seemed to know, Tucker froze his feet. The townspeople put him a flight to Fairbanks, where doctors amputated the heels and toes of both Tucker's feet. He returned to Eagle the following summer, blaming the loss of his feet on people who had helped him, such as Gary Howard, a Baptist missionary and hunting guide.

Howard earned his living with an orange Super Cub, the most recognizable plane in Eagle as it bounced off the town's grass airstrip and caught air over the Yukon several times each day in summer. Tucker had told Howard—and anyone else who would listen—that he wanted to shoot the plane. The day he followed through on his promise was his last day in Eagle.

After serving more than one year in jail for shooting the Super Cub, Tucker surfaced a few years later on July 4th. A woman driving the Elliot Highway north of Fairbanks called troopers after she had pulled over and saw Tucker in the woods. She called the troopers because she said that Tucker had worked the bolt action of his rifle while glaring at her. When troopers arrived, Tucker fired several shots with his .303 caliber rifle, disabling a trooper car and wounding a police dog. He surrendered to troopers after almost a full day of refusing to come out of the woods. He is now at Spring Creek Correctional Center in Seward, and is eligible for release in 2036, when he will be 85 years old.

Tucker's was an end-of-the-road story that could have been worse, as was the case in McCarthy in 1983, when Louis Hastings killed six people, and in 1984, when Michael Silka killed a state trooper and six other people near Manley Hot Springs.

As I sat on a stump outside the Pickerel Slough cabin, I wondered what tortured thoughts had swam through Dennis Tucker's mind out there, with most of his feet gone, a feeling he'd been done wrong, and all that time to stew. Another shiver ran through me. It was time to get back on the river.

As I was about to leave, I stepped inside the cabin one last time. From the debris, I picked up a letter from his mother, whose return address was on most of the boxes. She referred to him as "Den," and wrote that she had found some wooden crutches for him.

In a few seconds, my image of a vengeful madman disappeared. Dennis Tucker had a mother who loved him, just like me. Like me, he had read Coming into the Country and headed north trying to find a life that fit him. But something had gone wrong on Tucker's path, long before he reached the little cabin in Pickerel Slough, a place to which he would never return.

I set down the letter and pulled the cabin door closed behind me. I looked around the slough one last time, walked down the path, and slipped the canoe back into the water. As I paddled back to the Yukon, I tried to picture as a little boy the hairy man who froze his feet. All the while, I fought an incredible urge to look behind me.

I breathed a deep sigh when I reached the liquid boundary where the clear water from the slough mixed with the brown current of the Yukon. I dug my paddle in, pulled hard, and let the Yukon take me away.

CANIS LUPUS FAMILIARIS

As the spruce trees thinned and the trail wound up the low mountain pass, we saw fresh tracks, piddle marks, and scat from a wolfpack that had passed just hours, maybe minutes, ago.

Looking around the open landscape, it seemed the wolves would appear as moving dots somewhere on the horizon; the tracks were too sharp for them to be far. A scan of the countryside showed no wolves, but that test was only as good as my eyes. A better indicator was the nose of Canis lupus familiaris, and we had a few of them with us.

Our two dogs sniffed the tracks, and then poked their snouts in the air, inhaling molecules of the species they once were. Rather than sprinting in the direction of the scent, they stood there, staring down the trail, frozen like statues after smelling wolf for the first time.

If I had to read their minds from their actions, I'd guess that they had stumbled on something vaguely familiar but with a wild, scary edge. As we headed on toward the pass, the dogs trotted in single file behind us; it was not their usual spontaneous, scattered mode of travel.

As we skied on, I thought of the dogs whiffing the real thing out there, and how happy that made me to 1) be in a place where wolves roam, and 2) to have my own domesticated versions.

Dogs have been with Alaskans a long time, it seems. Scientists did DNA tests on bones of dogs frozen in Fairbanks permafrost at the time Columbus bumped into America. They said that those dogs' roots went back to wolves in Europe and Asia, rather than Alaska wolves. That meant dogs were probably at peoples' sides before they entered the New World via Alaska.

"Dogs may have been the reason people made it across the land bridge," said Robert Wayne of UCLA, a coauthor of the study, "They can pull things, carry things, defend you from nasty carnivores, and they're useful to eat."

I've never threatened to eat my dogs, but I've delayed their dinner as punishment for being bad. When they decide to run away together for hours, I fret at home until they come limping back into the yard, dirt on their muzzles from digging for voles. And I wish they wouldn't bark every time someone knocks on the door. It wakes up the baby.

On balance, though, those 50-pound creatures give more than they take. Daily walks with them are maybe more therapeutic for me than for them, and the image of their black bodies bounding through the nearby hay field is the definition of joy.

On backcountry trips, they are sometimes useful. Chloe charged at a black bear that came too close on one camping trip, and it scurried away. Once, as I tried to snap a leash on her collar, Poops noticed a black bear on a distant hillside, which was also on fire. Then she ran toward the bear, and the fire. That wasn't so useful.

Some people say dogs and wild places don't mix, and in some cases, they don't. Most National Parks don't allow dogs, because dogs kill things. My pair has ended the lives of a few red squirrels and voles. The dogs do some damage, but their ratio of things caught to things pursued is much lower than the super predator that is the domestic house cat.

Nothing against cats, but I am a dog person, and have been since I was a little boy. An editor once said he was "incredulous" at my claim that the main reason I hiked across Alaska one summer was to do something great with a great dog, but the logic was true for me. My life has changed since that long hike, almost 10 years ago; I'm no longer a bachelor living in a small cabin with a dog that is my constant sidekick. Now I'm married, we have a daughter, and we have two dogs.

They will never get the attention my old Lab Jane received, but I still love these animals and their personalities. Chloe came into my life as Jane was going out. She is a sensitive border-collie mix with the ears of a mule deer that set up like a gun site when she's alert. Those ears allow her to detect the subnivian world; she sometimes pounces like a fox for unseen voles under the snow. Inside the house, when she hears the words "go for run?" she employs a butt-spin move in which her rear ham swings like a boxing glove into our other dog's head, making everyone laugh except Poops.

Poops came to us from Golden Retriever Rescue with the name of Molly 5. Other families rejected her three times because she is a spaz. When we test-drove her for an overnight, I liked her because her tired groans reminded me of Jane, and because she climbed on the couch to take a nap with me. Poops always takes her passions one step too far—nosing into visitor's crotches when they enter our home, running over cliffs, bashing through spruce branches and coming back with a cuts on her face (self-inflicted injuries are her specialty). I enjoy her craziness because there's something so pure about it, and because she has so few years to be crazy.

Chloe and Poops have simple needs: They want to be outside, and they want to run. They're always up for an outing: Chloe once trotted a full 26 miles with me on a marathon training run, got a drink of water, then went out with Kristen for nine more. If you are wearing running shoes, you can wake both of them out of the soundest sleep at 3 a.m. and they won't be grumpy. They will be delighted.

Sometimes the trail is too much fun for the dogs. A few years ago, I took both heat-absorbing black dogs on a summer-solstice ridgetop hike from the Steese Highway to Chena Hot Springs. Water was scarce up high, it was 88 degrees, and the dogs pawed at every damp spot, snorting soil in a search for water. They ran a little lean on that trip, and I didn't enjoy it as much because I knew they were suffering.

The best dog days are the snowy-but-not-frigid ones like that March morning when we ran into the recent wolf sign. We were traveling between cabins in the White Mountains north of Fairbanks, with a 26-mile gap to cover that day. The dogs alternated days with their saddle pack, and that day was Poops's turn.

The dogs tailed us up the pass until the hand-size tracks of the wolves curved into a valley, and we kept going straight. Ptarmigan croaking near the treeless low pass lured the dogs off the trail into deep snow. They swam through it for a few seconds before giving up.

As we reached the top of the pass, gravity became our friend. We humans glided downhill without much effort, with the dogs sprinting to keep up after what was already a long day. A few more hours passed until we saw on a hillside the cabin we were aiming for.

We skied to the cabin and started a spruce fire snapping in the wood stove. I clicked Poops free from the doggie pack and scooped food into piles on the floor. Chloe savored every nugget, contemplating each one as she chewed it. Poops's food vanished in 10 seconds.

As the cabin slowly warmed and we ate our own dinner, the dogs treated us to one of the most satisfying sights there is: Trail-tired dogs stretched out on sleeping pads, twitching as they ran through dream landscapes with Canis lupus, the mother of them all.

DARKNESS TO LIGHT

It was the end of a crazy year, the year I couldn't get in touch with my sister in Manhattan for three days in September, the year she dabbed her eyes with a handkerchief one month later as we walked around the 14-acre hole that used to be the World Trade Center. It was the year of concrete dust, of the smell of hot metal and burned plastic, of a realization that someone hates you more than you thought possible.

After a few weeks of cold weather, a warm snap in late December provided a chance to get away from news of Osama bin Laden sightings and men with explosives in their sneakers. Temperatures held in the 20s in Fairbanks, so Kristen and I decided to drive north, way north, to the Arctic Circle. We would attempt a late December ski trip to an undeveloped hot springs that is nothing more than a few warm pools next to a frozen white river.

At the Klondike Inn in Fairbanks, I met with a trapper who works the country near the hot springs. Pausing from his cheeseburger and chips, he marked my topo map with a pencil, tracing the faint line of his trapping trail. His trail would make a good approach to the hot springs, though we would have to break our own path because low fur prices had discouraged him from running his trapline.

We drove north through a dead white world with two dogs, one borrowed and one belonging to us, in the back of the pick-up. Though insulated by distance from most of the changes that came with 9/11, we ran into a reminder on the Dalton Highway as floodlights lit up frosted spruce trees at a trooper checkpoint a few miles south of the Yukon River. A woman trooper wearing a black woolen cap squinted into the wind as she asked for our driver's licenses. We told her our plans, and she eyed our backpacks, skis, and dogs in the back of the truck. After disappearing into a hut for a minute, she handed me our licenses, satisfied that our intention was not to blow up the bridge that carries the trans-Alaska pipeline across the Yukon River.

As we drove across the bridge, with the Yukon cold and silent beneath us, I thought of how vulnerable that big pipe is, running 800 miles across Alaska, and how the crime of sabotaging a pipeline seemed like nothing now. The images of the twin towers falling in on themselves had played over and over in my mind since that day in September. I was born in Manhattan, and maybe a part of you always remains where you took your first breaths. Or maybe most people in America felt the same shock, anger, and vulnerability I did.

During my trip to see my sister, I saw what remained of two arrogant but undeniably grand structures: chunks of concrete and metal girders twisted like flower pedals, the metal facade of one of the towers sticking up like a skeleton, and the flexed arms of backhoes raising clouds of dust made of concrete, smoke, and vaporized people. But the city wasn't all grim; away from the destruction, New York was sunny and manic, full of people walking fast and talking on cellphones, the sidewalks bitter with the smell of grill-roasted chestnuts and the musk of the subway rising through metal grates.

Some sensations in the city were familiar: Navigating from Times Square to Battery Park with a plastic-coated city map gave a similar satisfaction to that felt when skiing from Nabesna to McCarthy by compass. Cutting through Central Park at dusk made my stomach tingle he way it does when I see a fresh bear track pressed into mud.

I strayed far from my birthplace about 20 years ago. I wanted a bit less out of life, and Kristen and I were now seeking some of the simplest things life had to offer—skis gliding on snow, snug backpacks, the thrill of finding old blazes on spruce trees, the promise of a soak in 110-degree water during the darkest days of winter.

The hot springs for which we aimed is about 13 miles south of the Arctic Circle, the imaginary line at 66 degrees latitude. Hills that blocked the view to the south assured we would never see the sun, though its presence below the southern horizon promised about five hours of twilight a day.

Kristen and I had only 12 miles to cover from the Dalton Highway to the hot springs, but we would have to make our own path through an exposed valley, along the side of Caribou Mountain, and down a few wind-scoured hillsides.

The Interior had experienced a snow drought in November and December, but two feet of wind-packed snow awaited us near the Arctic Circle. My skis broke through the crust with every step as we started off. We could have moved just as fast on snowshoes, but the country had filled our order for silence. When we paused, I could hear the pulse in my neck beating against my collar.

In three days of skiing, we never cast a shadow. We skied until we needed headlamps, stomped a flat spot for the tent, and then ate dinner in the dark. We crawled in our sleeping bays by 7 p.m. Snug and warm, we listened to the whisper of the wind through stems of dwarf birch and alder, and the snoring of tired dogs.

Our travel days began with a bluish light on the tent that gained strength until a person could read a map without a headlamp. My point-and-shoot camera, loaded with 200 ASA film, recommend the flash every time I used it.

A near-empty fuel bottle forced a decision when we were three miles from the hot springs. Because we soon would not be able to melt snow into water, we made the tough choice to retreat back toward the truck, the highway, and the rest of the world. The hot springs would have to wait, maybe for March or April, when there is enough sunlight to squander.

As we headed back toward the truck the next day, the big wind of the Kanuti River valley appeared, sandblasting us with loose snow as we marched on skis back to a log cabin owned by the trapper. After a few hours of squinting through snow pellets, we threw our gear inside the cabin and lit the oil stove. The wind rocked the cabin throughout the night, forcing spindrift through the logs and sprinkling powder on our sleeping bags.

The truck started the next morning after I chipped wind-driven snow from around the cooling fan. We threw our skis, poles, and packs in the back, coaxed the dogs in, and rolled onto the Dalton Highway.

As the engine warmed, we passed the granite tors of Finger Mountain, pink with early morning sunlight. For the first time on the trip, we saw the red ball of the sun, fulfilling the promise that Alaska was once again nodding toward the light, away from darkness. It was New Year's Day.

THE RESTLESS CORNER

The tide had turned in Disenchantment Bay. After hours of sucking in icebergs from Hubbard Glacier, Russell Fiord began spitting them through a narrow gap between glacier and cliff. Footsoldiers of ice marched toward our small metal boat.

Roman Motyka turned the boat away from the armada of ice and pressed the throttle. From a seagull's perspective, we looked like O.J.'s white Bronco followed by giant police cars.

I had never been chased by ice before, but I had never before traveled to the restless corner of Alaska where the southeast panhandle hooks on to the interior. There, amid mountains, glaciers, and ocean, the grand forces that shape Alaska move fast enough to alter your plans.

The icebergs that pursued us had fallen from Hubbard Glacier, which dips its tongue into salt water about 40 miles north of Yakutat, a town built on gravel the glacier left behind hundreds of years ago. Fed by fields of ice so immense that the glacier will rumble forward regardless of how warm the planet gets, Hubbard Glacier made headlines in 2002 when it bulldozed gravel into Gilbert Point, pinching off Russell Fiord's link to the sea and creating the largest glacier-dammed lake in the world. Before the gravel dam broke and changed the lake back into a fiord in August 2002, water rose six inches each day within the lake and threatened to spill into a world-class steelhead stream near Yakutat.

Hubbard Glacier follows no glacial code of conduct. While most other glaciers in Alaska are losing volume, Hubbard is gaining. Others are retreating; Hubbard is advancing. Most glaciers I have gotten close to in Alaska are static-looking hunks of ice and gravel. The retreat of Portage Glacier, for example, is impressive when you compare it to old photographs at the visitor center, but it does not trigger my adrenal glands.

My heart pumped a few extra beats per minute as we motored away from the icebergs of Hubbard Glacier. My partner in flight was Roman Motyka, who studies glaciers at the University of Alaska. He let me tag along on his study of the glacier in summer 2002, and the trip woke me up in a few ways.

Even though I live in the geographic heart of Alaska, I often forget the dynamic nature of my home. If I haven't felt an earthquake in awhile, I can get downright complacent about the stirring natural processes that surround me: The weak points in Earth's crust that slash through the state, ready to fail at any time and shake up our routines; the arc of puffing volcanoes that make up the Aleutian Islands; the rivers of ice clogging mountain valleys from the Brooks Range to Southeast.

I was beginning to understand the scale of these things while floating near the face of Hubbard Glacier. Fingers of blue ice 200 feet tall rose from the ocean, creating a wall about seven miles long where the glacier meets the sea. The glacier is so long that a Super Cub pilot needs one hour to fly its length, meeting its birthplace in the white world at the base of 19,551-foot Mt. Logan in Canada.

Ice at the blue face of the glacier probably fell as snow about 2,000 years ago, Roman told me. As chunks of the glacier fell to the sea, I thought of the air molecules now liberated after being trapped since the time of Christ's birth, and what ancient person had exhaled that air.

The icebergs stopped chasing Roman and I after we had retreated one mile from the gap between the glacier and Gilbert Point. The tidal current from the fiord weakened, and the icebergs meandered out into the bay. Roman turned the boat into the icebergs and picked his way back to Gilbert Point, where he had dropped off another glaciologist before the icebergs gave us the bum's rush.

When we returned to the glacier a few days later, Roman noticed a change. A new island of gravel existed near Gilbert Point. The gravel had been at the face of the glacier three days before. This meant the wall of ice had retreated several hundred yards since we were there last, part of a fall pattern of retreat that often follows the glacier's summer advance.

We looked out at the brand-new island, coated with resting seagulls. A seal circled the island, pausing to look up at the boat with the soft eyes of a Labrador retriever.

Roman took depth measurements between the new island and the glacier, mindful of the towers of blue ice that clung to the glacier with uncertainty. When I closed my eyes, the bay sounded like the plains of Kansas during a thunderstorm: Massive chunks of ice separated from the glacier and crashed to the sea. Smaller, car-size chunks sounded like gunshots when they hit the water.

"Keep an eye on that flake," Roman said, pointing to a blue sliver of vertical ice as large as an apartment complex.

His words seemed to will the ice into action, as we watched it lean in slow motion toward us. Roman turned the boat and gunned the engine even though we were a good distance from the glacier's face.

The ice flopped into the ocean with a roar. As we sped past the gravel island, I looked back to see—just 20 feet behind the boat—the splash from a chunk of ice the size of a softball that had been catapulted over the island.

Roman turned the boat once again, this time to face the glacier and the four-foot wave surfing toward us. The boat rode the wave up, then down, and Roman decided the day's work was done.

"Have we tempted fate enough times today?" he said.

A glacier had chased us away for the second time. As Roman got the boat on step, I tightened the hood of my rain jacket and watched Hubbard Glacier disappear into the mist behind us. Though I couldn't see them, I knew the pyramid of 18,000-foot Mt. St. Elias and a pancake-shaped glacier the size of Rhode Island were just to our left. I settled onto a metal seat for the long ride back to Yakutat with a new understanding of how Alaska reinvents itself, by the minute and the millennium.

CROWBERRY

It's a crazy windy day in the White Mountains when I decide to stop, veering off the main trail onto a familiar path that doesn't look quite so familiar anymore. On a 100-mile ski loop with my wife and my friend John in mid-March, I'm breaking for lunch near a snowy clearing that has a great view of the White Mountains, northwest of Fairbanks.

Today, I'm not enjoying the view. The wind is too icy, and the shelter that used to stand here, Crowberry Cabin, is gone.

Crowberry was a victim of the raging summer of 2004, when more than six million acres of Alaska burned. That's like losing Vermont in a forest fire. Though the wooden sign on the main trail pointing 25 yards to the Crowberry Cabin survived, a blank white clearing is where the cabin used to be. There's no stovepipe sticking up, nor any lumps in the snow. Even the outhouse has disintegrated. Sitting here on my sleeping pad, eating a bagel with cheese while the wind nibbles at my fingers, feels a bit like visiting a cemetery.

Crowberry was the only one of 11 cabins in the White Mountains National Recreation Area that the fire gobbled up. The porch of last night's cabin—Cache Mountain—is red with fire retardant splashed upon it by a tanker plane, but the cabin is fine. Firefighters with a D-9 Cat cut a beefy fireline to save Moose Creek cabin, where we'll stay tonight.

But Mother Nature nailed my favorite. It's strange to sit here surrounded by fingers of charred black spruce, some with orange needles clinging to them. They sure don't block the wind like a wall of milled spruce logs.

I miss that little cabin and its picture window that faced northwest, that window that was so good at pulling in the white light of late afternoon when you arrived after a long ski. With four bunks, a small woodstove, a Coleman stove and a lantern, the cabin had everything you needed out here and nothing you didn't.

I miss that little cabin because it had personality. Surrounded by the black spruce that killed it, Crowberry was like the dominant tree of the White Mountains: small and unassuming, but tough enough to stand up to a big wind. Its cheery little woodstove warmed the place fast, even at 20 below. Crowberry was about 30 miles from the road, so it didn't get the wear and tear of the closer cabins, the ones people use for day trips. Because its distance and the boggy terrain that led here made it reachable only in winter, the cabin's logbook held the entries of people like the marten trapper who would come out from Haystack mountain and warm himself here while setting up his line. I'd read his entries and think of him out here in the backcountry, alone in December's blue light, while most of Alaska's population was indoors.

The sharing is one of the things I like best about Alaska's public-use cabins, which the Bureau of Land Management builds, rents, and maintains out here and the state manages at other locations. I'll never toss a frozen marten under the seat of my snowmachine out here, but I know the guy who did always left the cabin clean. I never zipped out to Crowberry in less than two hours on an RMK-500, but those Air Force officers who did cut up a good stack of firewood before they left.

A few people leave trash behind, cut down live trees or don't pick up the poop from their dog teams, but they are the exceptions. For the most part, life at the cabins makes me believe that no matter how much I curse snowmachines when I'm eating their exhaust, I'm not so different from the people driving them. We sledders, mushers, skijorers and skiers are all out here for the same reason, because we're attracted to places that don't have pavement but do have wolf tracks.

I miss Crowberry because I felt like it was mine. I had a favorite place in the world when I was growing up, a plywood cabin my father, his friends, and my older brother built in 1975 on our seven-acre plot in Putnam, New York. There, I realized that I loved the smell of woodsmoke, that electricity was overrated, and that watching the woods through the open door of the outhouse could be the best minutes of the day. I still love that place my grandmother called "Instant Poverty," but it's five thousand miles from where I now live.

I've never owned a cabin in Alaska, but $25 gives me a deed to Alaska for 24 hours. It's like having a timeshare in the quietest acreage on Earth, within comfortable shelters that remind me of where I came from: the hiss of a Coleman lantern takes me back to playing cards with my dad and brothers until night turned to morning. The urge to stay in the sleeping bag when the fire has died is just as powerful at 42 as it was at 12. The smell of burning spruce makes me feel warm, as does the triceps workout of sawing logs on the porch. The logbooks always make good reading while sipping your hot drink, even if some phrases get a bit repetitive:

> *I'll be back.*
> *Northern lights rippling all night.*
> *This place is so beautiful.*
> *Thanks BLM.*

With my favorite little cabin vaporized into carbon particles that might be halfway around the world by now, the gnawing wind urges me to move on. I step into my bindings and think of the last time Kristen and I skied in here to Crowberry. We rented the cabin on April 9th, 2004, just before the snow melted and three months before Crowberry disappeared into smoky orange chaos.

With the snowpack disintegrating that April to the point where we had to leave the cabin in the coolness of 9 a.m., Kristen and I might have been the last people to look through that window at the limestone spine of the White Mountains. We might have been the last people to have swept the plywood floor, stacked kindling in the firebox, and put a pen to the green logbook that rested on the shellacked tabletop.

If we were the final people to sleep under that small roof, it was a privilege. Thanks BLM.

GUT FEELING

I'm sitting 20 feet in the air on two spruce logs suspended between parallel trees, watching the world go by. It's been a good show. A resident kingfisher has hunted the slough below, its blue Mohawk bristling with confidence. A boreal chickadee, choosing to remain here after all its fairweather cousins have headed south, has perched on a branch so close that I saw the forest reflected off the black bead of its eye. Beavers have left bubble trails after they dove, becoming sleek underwater forms easy to follow with binoculars. As an encore, a small, mysterious orange head cut a wake across the black water and then climbed to a log, where it shook like a dog and went on its way. I learned something I didn't know about the animal kingdom—red squirrels can swim!

The wildlife watching has been great above this backwater slough, a waterway beavers have sealed off from an Interior Alaska river. Problem is, I'm not here to observe small animals. I'm here to fill my freezer and the freezer owned by my friend John, who's here to help steer the canoe once it's heavy with moose flesh. I haven't harvested a moose in eight years, and I'm thinking that remaining up here in the air is not going to break the streak.

After seven hours in the spruce stand, I climb down and stretch my legs in the midday September sun, the musk of highbush cranberries heavy in the air. I slowly walk toward a grove of birch trees near the river, holding my breath to listen. Then, I stumble upon a moose.

This moose is a former one, now a pile of bleached bones picked clean by rodents and insects. It was a small moose, probably one that starved during a cold spell last winter and dropped right here. I see large teeth marks on some of the bones and for the first time feel a vague sense of uneasiness. Thinking it's just the clouds that have moved in and darkened the woods, I walk on to the main branch of the river.

At the bank of the river, which is narrow enough to throw a rock across, are a rotted blue tarp and half-buried beer cans. The trash brings back the unsettled feeling I felt at the bone pile. I turn to follow the riverbank upstream, which will take me back to our camp.

As I walk through tall balsam poplars, the undergrowth of prickly wild roses scratching at my pants, ravens scream from somewhere close. Gut pile, I think. Someone must have shot a moose nearby; the ravens are partying on the leavings.

Walking on, with more caution now, I see a plywood shack I didn't know was here. Abandoned years ago, its walls have airy curves where porcupines have gnawed the wood. Filled with porcupine dung, dark and dingy, the place gives me the creeps.

With the ravens still yelling, I walk back toward the river, cross a gravel bar, and step onto a small island, expecting to see ravens and maybe what they were squawking about. But the ravens have stopped chattering, and all I hear is the gurgle of the river.

Now I'm really spooked. My spidey senses are tingling, but I don't know why. A deep fear makes me not want to take a step, just listen. I hear nothing, except for the flow of the water.

I walk across the small island, pushing through willows that are too tall for my liking, rifle pointed ahead of me. The sense of dread is overwhelming. It seems like something bad is going to happen, but I know that's ridiculous. The logical side of me, the one that struggles to win every internal argument, reminds me that I've seen nothing to be afraid of. Loudmouth ravens may just be loudmouth ravens.

Passing through the gauntlet of willows, I come to a sandbar and see a fresh bear track pressed into the mud. My heart ratchets up a few beats. I turn back toward the slough and my tree stand.

I walk off the island, this time following the shoreline to stay out of the brush. I hike back across the gravel bar, taking a ramp back to the mainland that beavers established by dragging branches. I stop every few minutes on my walk back, listening, and sniff the air for that imagined gut pile. Nothing but the earthy smell of the river.

That night at camp, I tell John about my irrational fears on the willow island.

"Man, I got spooked today," I said between bites of dinner. "Might be something to that feeling," John said. "You never know what's going on in the woods."

The next morning, after another session off seeing no moose from the tree stand, we pack the canoe. I've failed again to bring home the moose steaks, but we've had a good camping trip, with a nice float ahead, about five river miles to John's waiting truck.

We slip the packed canoe into the river. Up ahead, I see the willow island that had me frozen in my tracks yesterday. My eyes sweep the shoreline for the plywood cabin, which I'll point out to John.

Instead of the cabin, I see something my brain has trouble decoding—two blond, hairy butts. Then, a dark brown body on the gravel, stained pinkish red, the color of torn flesh. As we drift by, a larger bear appears. Three grizzlies, a mother and two cubs, are yanking in concert on a moose carcass, which lays on the beaver ramp I walked up about 15 hours earlier.

In 10 seconds, as the current pulls us past the island, the scene disappears.

I turn in the canoe seat toward John.

"What did you just see?" I ask.

"Three grizzly bears eating a moose," he says. "I sort of wanted to beach the canoe and watch. Then I didn't . . . That makes the weekend, right there."

As we paddle on, each within our own thoughts, I replay a possible scene in my mind: the bears had pulled down the moose yesterday, attracting the ravens. I blundered close to the scene but somehow missed the three bears and the dead moose, its flesh too fresh to have any odor. Could those bears have been watching me in silence? Did they sniff a burst of my scent as I passed upwind? Was there something to that feeling of dread?

I'm guessing yes. I can't say what I happened while I moved through those willows, but I can say that some internal alarm made the small hairs on my neck stand up. I've had that gut feeling before, in other life situations, and paying attention to it has sometimes led to good things. This time, it might have altered my path ever so slightly, leading me out of the woods.

SANDS OF SHISHMAREF

Located on a narrow spit between the Seward Peninsula and the Chukchi Sea, Shishmaref is the Land of Sand. You knock sand off your shoes as you enter buildings, you blink it from your eyeballs after a gust of wind, you see it on rooftops and wonder how it got there. Tiny grains give way beneath the balls of your feet as you walk, making you feel like a car that's spinning out.

Shishmaref could be the only village in Alaska constructed on sand dunes, which is part of the reason reporters from CNN, the Weather Channel, and the New Yorker have taken flights here from Nome. The ocean is reclaiming the sands of Shishmaref, and writers and TV news reporters have described the village as one of the first victims of global warming.

I'm here to install a weather station for a University of Alaska project that will allow students to compare their weather to other schools on the Seward Peninsula, the nose of Alaska that points toward Russia. Storms hit Alaska's west coast with hurricane force every fall and winter, but sometimes it takes awhile for the rest of the world to hear about them. About 600 people live in Shishmaref, where October storms in 1997 and 2001 piled up seawater that ate more than 100 feet of the town's northern coastline. In 2002, villagers voted to move the town inland to Tin Creek. The Army Corps of Engineers estimates the move, if it happens, would cost $180 million.

With me on this trip is Dave Atkinson, a university scientist who's interested in the storms that affect people here. Alaska's west coast "is where Pacific storms come to die," Dave says. When a protective layer of sea ice isn't there to cap the ocean, the sea hammers places like Shishmaref, which has a maximum elevation of about 22 feet above sea level. Some scientists say that a smaller ice pack on the ocean, possibly caused by warmer air and sea temperatures, is threatening coastal villages like Shishmaref.

To get our own look at Alaska's poster village for global warming, Dave and I join Ken Stenek for a hike around town. Ken's a teacher here in Shishmaref whose roots go a bit deeper than most teachers attracted to the Alaska bush from the Lower 48. Since stepping off the plane in Shishmaref seven years ago from Washington state, Ken has married a local woman with whom he has had four children. He lives in a small house next to the school and uses a honey-bucket in lieu of the plumbing systems installed in the other 99 percent of American homes. Ken says he knew he was home shortly after arriving in Shishmaref.

"This place just sort of fits me," he says.

Ken walks us to where most of the action is, the northern border of town that recent storm surges have taken bites from. We walk on a seawall of boulders the size of state-fair cabbages, and Ken points to a dirty island surrounded by sea ice. "That's another seawall that didn't work," he says. "They built a fence around piles of sandbags, but the ocean just ate it up . . . and out here, under the ice, are big piles of cement blocks. Now they're underwater, a big boating hazard."

He points out the building that has caught our eye ever since we landed—a house tilted into the ocean, still intact but with its floorboards now at a 45-degree angle.

"That house was probably built in the 1950s. People abandoned it before it fell because the sea was creeping up," Ken says.

It's a jarring visual, and while it doesn't prove that our emissions of carbon dioxide are causing less sea ice to form, it shows that there's a lot less to Shishmaref than there was 50 years ago.

Ken takes us into the Shishmaref Native Store that's not far from the tilted house. In the windowless building, we see how far we are from most of America, and how important subsistence foods like bearded seal and berries are to local people. Browning lettuce wrapped in plastic sits in the refrigerator, oranges from California mold on the shelf, and a gallon jug of water from Anchorage costs $7.

Later, Ken walks us past Shishmaref's freshwater supply, a fenced-in area of about 15 acres where wooden snow fences create drifts that melt in spring and allow villagers to pump fresh water into their 1.3 million-gallon tank. This tiny reservoir of snowmelt is the only local water source other than collected ice. Here, it strikes me that Shishmaref is an odd place for a town.

It wasn't always a town. "The people along the sandy strand," or Tapqagmuit, lived for centuries in small villages that had been scattered along the spit that parallels the northern Seward Peninsula, according to cultural anthropologist Josh Wisniewski, who is visiting an elder in town. People didn't stay year-round at the present site of Shishmaref until about 1900, when Shishmaref became a trading center to support nearby gold mining.

Shishmaref is on a barrier island between the ocean and a large saltwater lagoon. Like all barrier islands, this one is a temporary feature, about the last place an engineer would choose to build a town.

A person could argue that, like New Orleans, Shishmaref is a place Nature wants to reclaim and eventually will, and it's a waste of money to try to defend the village from the sea. But Alaskans with that argument might first take a look at the fatal flaws out their windows. Some houses in Juneau sit in the runoff paths of avalanches. Fairbanks is a flood-prone city saved from the Chena River by an Army Corps of Engineers dam upstream. And seismologists will tell you that downtown Anchorage is one of the worst places in Alaska to be during a large earthquake, with clay soils beneath the city that act like a liquid when shaken.

Still covered by sea ice in late May, the gray ocean out there is the biggest threat to Shishmaref, which is not at its prettiest right now, as winter trash thaws from snowdrifts. The air smells like fuel when you're downwind of one of the aboveground tanks. Houses have wooden poles outside with seal meat draped over them that blackens as it dries in the icy wind. Rusted pickups that began life on some Lower 48 showroom floor die slowly in the salt air.

Today, people are outside enjoying spring sunshine. Kids ask us "What's your name?" and we tell them before asking theirs. As we turn to head back downtown, we bump into an older Shishmaref man working on his boat with his three sons.

"Tell President Bush he's got to do something about global warming," Fred, one of the sons who wears a "Native Pride" hat, says to visiting strangers.

Ken nods. "Shishmaref's one of the few towns in Alaska that votes Democrat across the board," he says.

Ken will introduce us to other residents before the walk is over, and they share their theories—a man who worked for the National Weather Service in Kotzebue says the number of storms has decreased in recent years, but they are less predictable. Another says the advent of four-wheelers coincided with the disappearance of vegetation on the beaches and has helped erosion. All agree that Shishmaref is not what it was.

And what will Shishmaref be in 20 years? The village might be much the same, if someone can figure how to hold back the sea. Or it might be another Alaska ghost town, with most of its structures abandoned or moved on an ice road to Tin Creek. In time, the swirling sands might drift over Old Shishmaref, a northern canary that didn't survive the coalmine of a changing world.

NEST FOR THE QUEST

The jingle of small metal snaps wakes me, reminding me that I am on the snow, and that the race is here.

Fifty-six cushioned feet pass so close to my head I can almost smell dog breath. The sled is next, stiff and banging on a path that seemed smooth on skis. Spruce shadows jump at the tent, then disappear as the yellow arc from the musher's headlamp sweeps past.

"Get up!" says a voice. "Good puppies."

Zack Steer sounds happy to see new trail, even though he is short on sleep. Maybe he has a tingle in his stomach when he thinks about the hills ahead and wonders whether he's pushing his rookie luck.

His cone of light moves on, towards the 3,000-foot pass the mushers call Rosebud. The trail behind him reverts to a faint white line etched into a dark curve of the globe.

I find my headlamp, switch it on, and shine blue light on my watch. It's 1:30 a.m. on the first night of the Yukon Quest sled dog race. I am stretched out in a small tent wedged between spruce trees, 10 feet off the trail. An embedded observer, I am camped on the North Fork of the Chena River, 100 miles into the musher's 1,000-mile journey. Because most of the racers are passing in the black of night, I will hear more of this race than I see.

Few of the mushers, if any, will see me. A fresh snowfall covered the tracks I left while skiing in from Chena Hot Springs Road a few hours ago. The fluffy white blanket has also camouflaged my small tent. When I skied to my nesting spot a few hours ago, the first mushers in the 1,000-mile race from Fairbanks to Whitehorse and their dogs were waiting out a layover at Angel Creek Lodge. Thirty-one of them left Fairbanks this morning, some of them gunning for a $30,000 first prize, all of them anticipating a grand adventure that starts each year around Valentine's Day.

"The Quest" first burrowed under my skin when I worked as a park ranger in Eagle, near the midpoint of the race. One winter I was part of a crew in Slaven's Roadhouse on the Yukon between Circle and Eagle. We warmed the place with a barrel stove and melted clear chunks of river ice in a pot. There, waking at all hours to serve mushers coffee and stew, I listened to Whitehorse musher Bill Stewart tell stories of the trail, his face orange in the candlelight, while his dogs slept on piles of straw outside at 30 below.

Those Yukon River nights set the hook, and since then I've read every newspaper story on the race and listened to every radio update. Though overshadowed by the Iditarod, the Quest has earned the reputation of being a tougher race due to greater distances between checkpoints and dog drops (an average of about 60 miles on the Quest, compared to about 45 miles on the Iditarod's northern and southern routes), steeper hills, and cold air that oozes thick into willowed valleys. You'll never see the winner of the Quest reported on CNN, and almost all of the mushers in this race have day jobs—newspaper editor, cab driver, lodge owner—where you might imagine their thoughts drifting to the trail.

That trail is alive with sound and motion tonight. Fingers of birch scratch the sky, pushed by a north wind that roars like the ocean and makes the ten-below air feel colder. I am a light sleeper, so over the lull of the wind I wake again to the jingles of brass snaps that announce the dogs of the second musher, Mark May.

"Yah!" May says, coaxing his dogs up a rise in the trail. It's 3:46 a.m.

May steps off his runners to jog the hill, and his lead dogs keep their noses on the trail. As Mark's cone of light disappears up the trail, I wish him luck. Years ago he let me drive a team of his dogs from his vet clinic in Fairbanks back to his home off the Chena River. In seven hours, he never said a word to his dogs and neither did I. His B team followed him on autopilot for forty miles, then up the steep chute trail that led from the river to his dogyard.

Behind Mark, a deep accent penetrates the wind, singing a song I don't recognize. As the musher dismounts to help his dogs up the hill, the jerks of the headlamp reveal his identity as the owner of Limp-a-long Racing kennel. William Kleedehn is a German expatriate living in Carcross, Yukon, who competes with a plastic prosthesis supporting his left leg from the knee down, the result of a motorcycle accident when he was 17. He is one of several Quest mushers born in continental Europe who have made mushing lives for themselves in northwestern Canada. Hans Gatt and Thomas Tetz are Kleedehn's neighbors of sorts, and it's easy to imagine them working and playing together, soaking up the open spaces that they couldn't find back home. When I worked as a park ranger on the Yukon, most of the vagabonds floating by on homemade rafts were from Germany, Austria, or somewhere else in northern Europe.

Kleedehn continues singing even as he limps up the hill, and then he is gone. The wind is still frothing through the treetops, and I'm glad to be in a sleeping bag rather than climbing to Rosebud summit. When they slide over that windy crossing and gravity pulls them downhill, mushers will be out of the basin that contains Fairbanks and North Pole and into the lonely northern country that drains into the Yukon River. Out there is the great unknown, and they will run into it head-on.

Hours later, when I'm packing up my tent, Kleedehn's race will be over. On the glare ice of the flats after the Rosebud descent, Kleedehn will crash to the ice and fracture his femur above his prosthesis. He will later refuse a helicopter ride and take a lift by pickup truck 100 miles to Fairbanks Memorial Hospital.

Mark May will also not see Whitehorse. In two days, fifty-below temperatures and gear problems on Birch Creek, between Central and Circle, will chill him to the point where he calls it quits at Circle. Zack Steer will continue on to lead his first Yukon Quest until the homestretch, when Hans Gatt will outsprint him into Whitehorse.

After stuffing my tent into my backpack, my Yukon Quest experience concludes with a surprise invite to the nearby cabin of new friends Jim and Mabbel Morgan for coffee (while setting up camp in the dark, I didn't know their cabin was close), and a daylight ski towards Rosebud on the Quest trail after running into a few members of the Fairbanks ski club.

I end the day soaking in the outdoor pool at Chena Hot Springs. Feeling the warm water pull the chill out of my bones, I stand against hot rocks and look to the north. Twilight reddens the hills of spruce, birch and aspen. Beyond that quiet horizon, 31 people and hundreds of dogs move on, pushing deeper into the Great Unknown.

NIZKI, POPULATION 1

From a bench of tundra on Nizki Island, I key the handheld radio.

"Are the bird guys still on the island?" I ask.

Negative, you're the only one on the island, says Billy, the captain on duty. *You can't say that too often.*

No, you can't. This Aleutian island is all mine, at least for another hour or so. I've gotten to this faraway spot as a volunteer for the Alaska Maritime National Wildlife Refuge. Today was the final day of searching the island for Aleutian goose nests, and we finished our last grid across the island in early afternoon. When a group of others returned to the ship, I asked if I could wander for a while.

"Sure," said Jeff Williams, a biologist with the refuge. "Just take a radio. Hike to a high point and give us a call every hour so we know where you are."

Roger that, I said, heading off into bumpy hills of tundra and grass, happy for the chance to explore and for a break from group living. For the past two weeks, a dozen of us have lived in close quarters on the refuge's ship, the *Tiglax*.

Now, I've got 1,700 acres to myself. Nizki, closer to Japan than to my home in Fairbanks, is a wedge of tundra, grass and volcanic rock pointing toward Russia. Less than three miles long, the wedge tapers from a quarter-mile wide at its eastern end, the one that points back toward Alaska and the rest of the U.S. Nizki is one of the Near Islands, the last specks of volcanic Alaska before Russia takes over.

What to do with your own island? You could backtrack to near the beach and root around the lush green middens, the beachfront catacombs of aboriginal people fertilized by the bones of seals, otters, fish, and the people themselves. Or you could run the around the island on the beaches, 12 miles to a lap.

Instead, I plop down on a comfy bed of native grasses, crow-berry, and other tundra plants. The sun sneaks through the clouds, a rare treat, and warms me on a slope that's sheltered from the wind. From my Aleutian easy chair, I watch a song sparrow—the jumbo Aleutian version—singing and chasing its mate. Gulls chuckle as they cut the air like kites, and puffins shoot out of cliff side burrows like orange bullets. The air smells like the sea, with an occasional whiff of ammonia from rocks whitewashed with guano. This place is alive, but not with people. As far as I know, there are 14 people floating in Pinnacle Cove a bit south of here, and no one to the north until you top the pole and start going south again toward Scandinavia. Right now, Nizki Island has a population of one.

Here's a good place to contemplate the metaphor of man as island, but the honking of geese overhead distracts me. The hundreds of goose nests on this island, warm to the touch as you replaced the mother's down after she flushed, are evidence that the species with the big brains and opposable thumbs might have done something right here. Even since we were born, we've heard how species have gone extinct because of the actions of man. Filter those stories through the brain of a little boy and he might conclude that humanity is not a good thing for the planet. That negative feeling towards his species might be reinforced when he hears about times like about the day in 1911 when American fur traders dropped a pair of arctic foxes off on the beach here. That pair became hundreds, and, to survive, those foxes preyed on the island's birds with such efficiency that the ground nesters went someplace else, if they could find someplace else. Some, like the Aleutian goose, disappeared—from the planet, many bird-people thought—because Russian and American fur traders released foxes on the beaches of almost every other Aleutian Island too.

But Aleutian geese, smaller cousins of the Canada goose, now fly overhead by the dozens, and biologists counted more than 400 nests here on Nizki in the survey that ended today. The 1984 nest count was zero.

The recovery of the goose is due to in part to a gutsy biologist named Bob Jones who in 1962 bashed his wooden dory onto the shore of Buldir, an island 100 miles east of here that was too remote and its beaches too rocky for fur trappers. There, he found a few hundred Aleutian geese. Jones's protégés, including Vernon Byrd, now on the *Tiglax* one-quarter mile away, captured birds from Buldir and carried the young to other islands like Nizki.

For the birds to live here, the foxes had to go. Biologists and professional trappers hired by the refuge have been trapping and killing foxes since the late 1940s. A trapper killed the last fox on Nizki in 1976.

After the relocation of hundreds of geese here, a sea-otter biologist saw a pair of geese with goslings on Nizki in the summer of '87. The geese had finally stuck, and they've moved in ever since.

If you're not an arctic fox, it's a happy story: Today's residents of this island are the same species that were here before Vitus Bering sailed by in the St. Peter in the 1740s. Turning back the clock isn't possible in most places on Earth, but it seems to have happened on Nizki.

My time is dwindling on this lovely green island. Dinner's on in the galley at 6:30, and if I don't make it back on the *Tiglax* by then, people wait. I get up from my tundra nest and feel bad for making a goose scurry off. *I'll be out of your feathers soon enough.* But first there's something I want to do.

I walk on spongy vegetation and descend to the rocky eastern point of the island. There, with the ocean at my feet, is just what I'm looking for. In a knee-deep canyon between rocks, small waves rush in from the north and the south, meeting in the middle.

I roll my hip boots all the way up and tie them off to my belt. Walking carefully on barnacles and slippery kelp, I step into the little canyon, facing east. With good footing on the black sand below, I watch two of the world's great oceans rush in and wet me to the knees, then retreat in sizzling foam.

One foot in the Bering Sea and one in the Pacific Ocean, I snap a picture as the oceans collide over my boots. After about

15 minutes, when the novelty wears off, I think about dinner again. I turn around and step toward the island of Nizki, population zero.

CONTINENTAL DIVIDE

Wales is the farthest-west village on the Seward Peninsula, on the tip of Alaska's nose that points away from America and toward the Old World. On a clear day like today, you can see the hulk of Big Diomede Island, Russia, floating out there on the Bering Sea.

Cold wind nibbles through our jackets as Dave Atkinson and I lift our gear into a four-wheeler trailer for the short trip to the Wales school. We are here to install a weather station, part of a university project. The bearings of the anemometer will get a workout here, because Wales' average wind speed is 18 mph.

As we take a bumpy ride through a tunnel cut through a snowdrift over Wales' only street, I steal a few glances upward at the hillside in front of us, a rocky mound with black tors cutting through it like teeth. Where the ridge drops into the cold ocean is Cape Prince of Wales, another Alaska spot named for a man who would never see it. That spot is also the northern end of North America's spine, the somewhat continuous ridge that runs all the way from the Panama Canal to Alaska—the Continental Divide.

The divide is the backbone that marks the theoretical point where a drop of rain falling on one side will find the Pacific and another a few feet away will migrate to the Atlantic. The definition works for most of the continent, but is not as neat in Alaska. Instead of running north-south as it does for most of its trip over the continent, the divide here runs mostly east-west, separating watersheds that drain northward to the Arctic Ocean from those that drain westward to the Bering Sea and southward to the North Pacific.

In Alaska, the Continental Divide extends from the far eastern Brooks Range along the highpoints of those limestone peaks until it drops out of the Brooks to the headwaters of the Kobuk River. From there, the divide bends south on a drunken path until it makes a westward run across the Seward Peninsula. For the first time since Panama, it touches salt water right here in Wales.

Though the divide runs across the width of the state, not many people in Alaska talk about it, because the imaginary line doesn't intersect many places traveled by people. The Haul Road from Livengood to Prudhoe Bay is the only highway to cross the Continental Divide. Long-distance truckers perhaps notice the geographical milestone the most, when they finish the steep pull up Atigun Pass and smell the asbestos from the brake pads of trucks in front of them as they pitch down the other side.

In Wales, we are a long way from big trucks. The only street is a few hundred yards long, and the village is among the smallest I have seen. Only 152 people live here, according to the 2000 census. Many more lived here before the 1918 flu arrived with the contagious cough of a dogsled driver. After he carried the disease into Wales in November 1918, 178 of 396 people died the following week.

Today, Wales is quiet, with few people outside, as Dave and I install the weather station on a school outbuilding made of lumber imported from elsewhere. There are no trees in Wales, but for me this place has a more comfortable feeling than other tundra villages, though I can't place why.

With our install complete, Dave and I have the rest of the night for whatever we want. It is early summer and there is no fog, so it's a perfect night for a walk.

We are soon off for the Continental Divide, climbing spongy tundra toward the rock-covered ridge.

On the way, we come across the grave of Harrison Thornton, marked by a white obelisk. Thornton, a Christian missionary, came here in 1890. He feared locals would someday kill him. His instincts were correct. They murdered him on Aug. 19th, 1893. Carved into his white stone, which overlooks the Bering Sea: *A good soldier of Christ Jesus.*

Dave and I continue up the ridge. The tundra gives way to rock, and the walking becomes excellent, making me think of the possibility of a Continental Divide Trail across Alaska, like the one that exists from Montana to New Mexico.

But improved trails and other changes are not racing to the western Seward Peninsula. A look westward from our vantage point shows two wind turbines standing over the lake-pocked flats at far end of the village. My friend Mari Shirazi is one of the engineers who designed a wind-diesel power project for

Wales a few years back. The rotors are now static and unmoving, like the pedals of a flower. The wind/diesel system once worked well enough that people in Wales could shut off the diesel generator to power the village about 40 percent of the time, but the straight generator system is much easier to fix than the wind-power system, which broke a few years ago.

Sometime after midnight, a ghostly figure bounds through the rocks ahead of us. It's an arctic hare, which looks giant compared to a snowshoe hare and on the barren black landscape. We stop to watch the exotic creature bound away to another pile of rocks. Just then, I realize there's a slight downslope ahead of us.

"This is it, Dave. We're on the divide."

Dave tries to take a photo of me with a foot on tilting rocks on either side of the Continental Divide with Russia in the background, but the light is too low for his camera. We give up on the photo and hike upward through the cold evening light. The wind picks up as we ascend the rocky ridge and are now the tallest things between the Chukchi and the Bering seas.

Frozen in this moment of time, we are perhaps the only people standing on the divide as it runs through Alaska. Someday, Alaska might be populated enough for a groomed trail to become a reality, and it would be a great one, traversing from the high peaks of the Brooks Range to the upper Kobuk and Koyukuk country to the mysterious interior of the Seward Peninsula, which has its own Death Valley. But right now, I like that we're the only ones on this ridge in the blue light of the early morning, and that the Continental Divide is ours for the night.

MY ALASKA BROTHER

My friend Andy sits down on the bus, then remembers his Ice Kings, the heavy winter boots he wore to survive a ride down to Anchorage in my Subaru. Because he doesn't want to carry ten-pound boots on his back for 350 miles, he rushes off the bus and hands the Ice Kings to a friend. Snow melts from his bare feet as he walks back onto the bus.

Andy pulls on his ski boots as the bus rolls toward Knik Lake, the starting point for the Iditarod Trail Invitational from Knik to McGrath. Andy decided last-minute to do the race. I had signed up months before. His presence here on the bus has changed the race's dynamic for me. I had envisioned a solitary journey with hours of quiet contemplation of the changes coming in my life. Now, the closest thing I have to a brother in Alaska is here—a guy who once shared his last three almonds with me when we were running out of food, a guy who was as sad as me when my dog died, a guy whose Mom has mailed treats for us to village post offices.

We know we'll be traveling together, and when we reach the Knik Bar we know this won't be much of a race. The heavy snow falling outside has taken the speed element out the Invitational, so we sit back at a table and watch nervous bikers, walkers, and skiers waiting for the call to the starting line on Knik Lake.

The trail—six inches of new fluff over icy hardpan—is not good for skate skiing. We shuffle up the Iditarod trail, moving off the path to let walkers pass. In the past, I would have hated this, called it a Death March, and I would have resented Andy for not hating it, for being the steady, satisfied person he is.

But maybe he's rubbing off on me. Through the years we have been through so many hours of marching on cold snow, so many minutes of feeling the wind bite through gaps in clothing. This time, I know it may be a while before I do a similar trip with Andy, so I've decided not to allow the details that are out of my control—just about everything except moving forward—eat at me.

Later, Andy will call this the "Ned Junior Tour," because my wife Kristen is pregnant with our first baby, and things will change, people tell me. I believe those people, so I went into this journey with no expectations. I'm taking what the trail gives, realizing the trail doesn't owe me anything, and being thankful for what I get. Andy was in that mode a long time ago; I wonder if he was born that way.

"There is absolutely no one like Andy on the face of this earth. No one. He is one in six billion," a friend, Frank Wolf, emailed me after mountain biking from Dawson City to Nome with Andy. Examples of Andy's uniqueness are there from the start of the Iditarod Trail Invitational.

Approaching the Alaska Range midway into the race, at Shell Lake Lodge, we stop for the night. Zo, the proprietor, watches Andy stumble a bit as he walks into the lodge.

"You look sore," she says, making the plausible assumption that Andy is stiff from the trail. She doesn't know he has limited movement in his right leg after he broke his neck skiing off an icy trail into a tree about 15 years ago. Back then, some doctors said he wouldn't ski again. He has since covered thousands of Alaska miles by his own power, using incredible amounts of energy to overcome muscles that no longer fire as they once did.

In the morning, Zo cooks us breakfast before we hit the trail. She sets a stack of pancakes in front of Andy.

"Do you have any mustard?" he asks.

She laughs.

"You guys are all so eccentric. Like the Italians last night. They mixed their beers with 7-Up."

Andy squeezes mustard on his pancakes and smiles like he couldn't possibly be happier. It's quite a contrast to other racers who are sleeping two hours a day rather than the eight we are sleeping. We see some of them at checkpoints holding their heads in their hands, saying they are "shattered," and looking like they couldn't possibly be more miserable.

Andy's upbeat attitude helps him overcome a constant need to eat. I used to cringe inside at the sound of Clif bar wrappers crinkling nonstop behind me, but after logging so many trail miles with Andy, I trust him. We have only run out of food once, and that was because of a poor navigational decision by me (and he still shared the three almonds he found in a corner of his pack).

It's better not to worry. Instead, I think of the mountains surrounding us, look at the animal tracks in the snow and hum tunes that correspond with our trail pace.

"We're livin' right, man," I say at a snack break.

"Yeah, this is great," Andy says.

This trail, the first third of the Iditarod, is new to me, but not to Andy. He mushed it twice in the Iditarod and is the only person to attempt the race from Knik to McGrath on skis more than once (this is his fourth time). He shares a lot of memories out here.

Crossing a frozen swamp outside Finger Lake, he points out the spot of last year's "death bivvy," where he curled up in his sleeping bag with a fever until other racers got him help.

"This is where Roberto (a walker nicknamed 'the Italian Moose') picked me up with one arm and stuffed me into my bivvy sack."

Andy had to scratch then, taking a flight out of Finger Lake. This year is much better; he didn't start the race sick and there will be no death bivvy for either of us.

I never get tired of his stories as we ski along. Nor do I get tired of going the right way.

A few days ago, we were surprised to see Steve Reifenstuhl of Sitka sitting at the first checkpoint. Steve walked the 350 miles to McGrath last year in just over four days; this year he took a wrong turn before the first checkpoint, walked miles out of his way, and scratched. I was tempted to follow the same marked trail, but Andy knew it was the Junior Iditarod trail. I would have agonized over the decision without him.

It used to irk me that Andy's trail sense was so bombproof, but now I feel privileged to have such a trail guide. He has removed from this trip the despair of being lost; that's no small thing.

As we ski one last day into McGrath through sunshine and warm 20-degree air, I look at Andy and wonder what this trip would have been like without the trail sage in front of me repeating his infinite V-1 stroke to the right. I'm a solitary dude, no doubt about it, but eight hours with my own thoughts out here would have been plenty. The 100 trail hours beyond that would have been lonely and forlorn, no matter how lovely Dalzell Gorge was by moonlight.

At the finish line on a snow-covered street in McGrath, we stop and give each other a big hug. I squeeze Andy's extra-lean torso through a few layers of damp nylon. I hold on for a few extra seconds, super tight, trying to preserve the feeling of this nine-day journey. It's one of our best ever. We accepted each other's quirks and didn't let the good moments pass without mentioning them. Though I feel great, I also feel a bit blue, because maybe we'll never do this again. Before I let Andy go, I say a silent "Thank you" that I was able to once again share the trail with my Alaska brother.

SIGNS OF MAN

Wandering a hillside above the Charley River, I saw something on the tundra that stood out in the jumble of green and brown plants. A shriveled yellow balloon had fallen to Earth and draped itself over a bush. I walked over, picked it up and saw a tag, telling the finder the balloon was a weather experiment.

I wasn't that happy to be the finder. There on the small mountain in the middle of Alaska, I was in the most remote place I'd ever been. The closest road was 150 miles away; the Charley River was 2,500 feet of bumpy tundra below me, so I was far enough to be out of range of the occasional rafter out to stretch his legs. I had arrived there by helicopter, while working for the National Park Service, and in the two weeks

I was camping there had seen no other sign of people on the ground.

The discovery of the weather balloon came somewhat early in my Alaska experience, when I saw things from a different perspective than I do now. Back then, I traveled into the quiet places with the expectation that I would see wolf tracks; boot tracks pressed into river mud would ruin my day. When I walked through one of those deep backcountry places, I'd always try to leave behind none of my own tracks as a courtesy to the next visitor. I wanted to create the illusion that whoever followed was the first person to step foot there, because that feeling was so important to me.

I waged my own little war on the man-sign out there. I once kicked over rock cairns someone had built to mark the way on a somewhat popular but remote trail. I still remember the deflated feeling that came later on that trip when I found a Teva sandal someone had dropped at a river crossing. I wanted pristine. That's what Alaska was about for me.

But I rarely found pristine. Always, there would be a Super Cub strip outlined by rocks on top of a hilltop it'd taken three days of hiking to reach, or a line of alders marking a Cat trail someone had pushed into a remote drainage to follow a streak of gold. The country almost never met my expectations that I would see nothing but nature.

I began to get the big picture a few years ago when I picked up a book by Alfred Brooks, the namesake of the Brooks Range. In the book, the geologist and explorer described to his bosses the state of the state in 1906, after he had completed some difficult traverses. Only about 60,000 people lived in Alaska then, about a tenth of today's population, but Alfred Brooks found signs of man wherever he went.

"The more venturous prospector found no risk too hazard-ous, no difficulty too great, and now there is hardly a stream which has not been panned by him, and hardly a forest which has not resounded to the blows of his ax," Brooks wrote. "Evidences of his presence are to be found from the almost tropical jungles of southeastern Alaska to the barren grounds of the north which skirt the Arctic Ocean."

And if a person wants to dig a little deeper, he or she can find more in the layers below. John Smol of Queens University in Ontario has found high levels of nutrients in lakes of the Canada's high arctic. He thinks whalebone structures built by people, the descendents of ancient Alaskans, are enhancing the lakes. Those former Alaskans abandoned the spot more than 400 years ago.

The deeper you dig out there, the more you find, like the 1,000-year old slab of blubber a boy found while rooting through Gambell's old town site. Someone has always been there before.

Most of the stuff you stumble upon in Alaska now is due to the capillary pull that drew gold seekers up even the smallest creeks. The hills north of Fairbanks had people crawling all over them, and a railroad serviced towns like Vault and Golden City, which are hard to find today if you're standing on them. Even the hills of Glacier Bay, vacated by glaciers not long ago, have mining tunnels, complete with ore cars and a system of rails. Gold dredges the size of apartment buildings slowly decompose in some of the more hard-to-reach drainages in Alaska. Forgotten men and their machines carried them in pieces over oceans, on trains, and down rivers. They reassembled the dredges while swiping at mosquitoes in quiet country that, for a few decades, wasn't so quiet.

Now, as long as I have silence, the stuff out there doesn't bum me out so much. While caribou hunting by myself in the northern foothills of the Brooks Range a few falls ago, I saw through binoculars a lone ski pole sticking up from the tundra. I walked over to the pole and wondered who had left such a tool behind, making the effort to plant it in the tundra and leave it in a standing position. Then I saw the company name and wondered how the ski pole had made it from Scandinavia to the edge of a melt pond high in Alaska. Without any caribou to sneak up on and getting lonely after a few days by myself, I welcomed the distraction.

Old-timey trash is always kind of fun. One of my favorite things is to stumble upon the remains of an old log cabin and try to figure out who built it, when the cabin emerged from the surrounding forest, and what it was like to live there. I see the old garbage middens with the always-present Hills Bros. Coffee tins, and imagine drinking a cup, cut with concentrated milk, after a day of working the tailings pile.

Contemporary garbage is almost always a bummer out there, but sometimes I'm giddy to see it. On a ski trip from Kotzebue to Kobuk a few springs ago, my friend Andy and I had been moving for about 10 hours when our trail forked in three directions. Each prong was about the same width and each had about the same amount of sno-go travel. Points like this often cause big-time anguish: choosing the wrong fork costs time, food, and morale.

Andy and I stopped at the trail junction and looked around. We both spotted salvation at the same time: Someone had bent over a branch and shoved a Pepsi can onto it. Andy and I smiled to each other without saying a word. We turned toward the can and followed it to Ambler.

MEMORIAL DAY, ATTU

Sixty-one years ago, guys who hadn't pulled off their wet leather boots for two weeks were snuffing the last charge of enemy soldiers on this island of white mountains. Today, I slip into my running shoes and out the door to explore Attu.

I've made it to the farthest west island in Alaska—closer to Tokyo than it is to the state capital—as a volunteer for the U.S. Fish and Wildlife Service. Biologists are capturing ptarmigan here and boating them to a new home on Agattu, about 30 miles away. Today I'm taking time off to discover the island away from the U.S. Coast Guard station where we've been living for a week.

Heading out of the Coast Guard building, home to about 50 Coasties who spend a year here and then get to choose their next assignment, I jog a few steps into the wind. Tennessee sprints to join me. Tennessee is a brindle mixed-breed mascot of the Coast Guard who keeps the rat population down and barks at visitors. Today, he's in the mood to move. Good. I'm happy for the company.

With snow sticking to the shoulders of Terrible Mountain (named by GIs) to the north, the temperature on Attu is in the 40s, about 20 degrees warmer than the late spring of 61 years ago. On May 11, 1943, more than 11,000 U.S. soldiers landed on the island in an attempt to drive out 2,650 Japanese that had invaded Attu the previous June, part of a diversion to pull American troops from the South Pacific, according to Brian Garfield, author of *The Thousand-Mile War*.

This May seems a kinder time to be on Attu. The spears of rye grass that make walking the hills a quad-burning affair in mid-summer are just sprouting. Snow bridges still cover some of the creek crossings in the passes and there's no need for sunblock or bug dope. A mosquito would need big pecs to resist the blow toward New Zealand.

I run along an old Army road that parallels Massacre Bay, named not for one of the three World War II American points of invasion but for a Russian landing party's murder of 15 native Aleuts here in 1745. As Tennessee and I pass the remains of American wharfs on Massacre Bay, the thought strikes that no Natives have lived here since the Japanese shipped them to Hokkaido in World War II. The sea's riches would make for relatively easy living here, but no one will ever live on this National Wildlife Refuge again; except for the Coast Guard men who will be here as long as the LORAN transmitter is running.

From Massacre Bay I turn inland, following the steps of invading GIs from Florida, Georgia and Wisconsin who were pressing down muskeg in a part of America familiar to none. Trained by staging mock attacks on California beaches, they wore uniforms better suited for the South Pacific as Japanese snipers in the foggy hills pinned them in the muck. At the end of the battle, 549 men died and more suffered severe cold injuries and exposure (1,200) than were wounded by the Japanese (1,148).

"The soldiers' feet perspired freely in their high leather blucher boots, and when the perspiration froze, frostbite immediately attacked their toes," Garfield wrote in *The Thousand-Mile War*. He added that three-week battle here forced the military to develop better cold-weather gear. "In the next two years' global fighting, the experience of Attu would save thousands of limbs and lives. It did not, however, save hundreds of Attu veterans from amputation."

With Tennessee loping along shotgun, I run uphill to where the road disappears under the remains of winter's snowpack. Testing the snow with a few footsteps, I find it consolidated enough to float my running shoes. Tennessee and I head on toward Jarmin Pass, a gap between 2,000-foot hills where the Japanese prevented three invading American divisions from joining up for two weeks. The only battlefield relics at the top of the pass are rusted posts that once held barbed wire and the depressions in the snowy tundra dug by bomb or bayonet. I take a long look toward the white pyramid of Attu Mountain, the high point of the island at about 3,000 feet, and turn back toward Engineer Hill. Tennessee flushes yakking ptarmigan from the treeless tundra.

As I run, I notice steam coming from the hillside and wonder if Attu has sprung a leak. Getting closer, the steam shows itself to be a waterfall that the Aleutian wind is blowing back uphill. The gusts shove me off balance as I move over the snowfields.

As I start up Engineer Hill, a stone monument within four metal fenceposts pulls me near. I wonder if it's a grave at the same time I realize I've probably stepped on dozens of unmarked graves today. A sign on a plaque indicates the spot where Colonel Yasuyo Yamasaki, the Japanese commander on Attu, died while making a desperate charge up Engineer Hill. As Garfield wrote in *The Thousand-Mile War*, Yamasaki and fewer than 800 remaining Japanese soldiers had heard that the Japanese evacuation fleet would not be coming for them, so the colonel made the decision to charge through the American line at Engineer Hill, capture American howitzers there and turn them on the Americans. His banzai rush almost worked, but a group of surprised roadbuilders, cooks and staff officers turned the Japanese away before they reached the big guns. Later that day, 500 Japanese held grenades to their chests and pulled the pins. Soon after the mass suicides, Yamasaki charged one last time, sword in hand. An American soldier killed him with a .30 caliber bullet, right here, and the battle for Attu was pretty much over. Only 28 Japanese remained for the Americans to take prisoner.

Looking at the date on Yamasaki's memorial, I realize he fell on this spot on this very day, 61 years ago. On May 29th, 2004, I hear only the honks of Aleutian Canada geese and the wind whipping the brown tangles of last year's rye grass.

I move on through a thickening fog, hoping to find the Japanese War Memorial. My sneakers are squishy and wet, and my feet would be cold if I stopped moving. I sidestep yawning trenches and the buckling wooden platforms that were once floors of Quonset huts.

Through the mist, there it is, a futuristic titanium star, tall as a telephone pole, attached to the hill by the Japanese government in 1987 to honor the dead on both sides. The wind hums a spooky tune through the prongs.

It's been four hours since Tennessee and I left the Coast Guard station. I leave the war memorial and head back into the wind. Tennessee shakes water from his fur, then follows. We cross over a network of trenches dug by the Japanese overlooking Massacre Bay. With a sniper's view, I can imagine the smell of burning diesel and the sight of American landing craft cruising toward the black sand beach.

Slaloming through snow to reach the flats of East Massacre Valley, I cross a rotting wooden bridge to reach the site of Little Falls cemetery. Here, 3,000 Japanese and Americans are buried, eight to a trench. Though the cemetery sign is gone, and the crosses are missing too, I pause for a few minutes here, on this Memorial Day.

How could such a lovely, lonely island no bigger than Anchorage have been a place of so much bloodshed less than a lifetime ago? The swirling wind has no answer for me. I yell for Tennessee, take a long look back at the graveyard, and start running toward the Coast Guard barracks.

THINGS THAT GO BUMP

Rain falls at 10:38 p.m., and the glow of a candle next to me is the only light for many square miles. I am alone in a plywood cabin, waiting for a noise in the night.

I'm as scared as a boy alone in a tent for the first time, and I can't believe my luck. The hunting guide has left me on a lonely stretch of a river that empties into the Yukon. A moose-hunting client cancelled his hunt because of heart trouble, so my boss, Len, decided to leave me alone at the little green cabin while he returned to his other hunters at a larger camp downriver. He said he would return with the next client in eight days.

"You can scout the area for moose," he said. "Use the canoe to get a feel for the country."

Employed as a packer, I have for the last month carried the meat of sheep and moose shot by men from outside Alaska who have paid thousands of dollars for the privilege. I have cooked for them, carried their gear, and listened to stories of animals they have killed.

I've had my fill of hunting stories. Now, and much of the time, I prefer solitude to company. I recognize that hungry feeling inside when I need a dose of alone.

That feeling melted away as Len's Supercub rattled west over hills of birch and muskeg early this morning. In the wake of the plane, I felt a silence so powerful I opened my mouth to quiet my breathing, savoring the gurgle of the river.

I'm not the only mammal in this large green-and-brown patch of Alaska. A grizzly bear shares my space. Yesterday, before Len left me at the cabin, we repaired a hole the bear had torn in the plywood wall. The hole was as large as a basketball hoop. Once the bear chewed and clawed its way through layers of glued wood, it sampled everything inside, coating the floor with cooking oil and other hard-to-remove ingredients. To patch the hole in the wall, we tacked a square of plywood spiked with nails like a porcupine.

I met the cabin invader this afternoon. I was floating the river in the canoe, tossing a Pixie at a slough in hopes of a pike dinner. I saw movement on a willow and spruce hillside, and picked up my binoculars.

The grizzly was running uphill with good speed, blond and beautiful, shoulders rippling. I drifted close to a riverbank that filled the binoculars with willows, and I lost the bear. I made a mental note to tell Len on our 10 p.m. radio check.

The river arced to the north to where a gravel bar and cutbank pinched the muddy water to a mere 5 yards across. As I rounded a bend, the bear was there at the squeeze, hunkered on the gravel bar. With the fluid motion of a panther, he paced toward the approaching canoe.

The riverbank crumbled beneath his heavy steps. He stumbled, but kept advancing, closing the distance between us to 50 yards.

I thought of the large-caliber rifle tied to the middle seat of the canoe, out of reach. I looked at the round face of the bear; it rumbled along the riverbank and sniffed the air so hard it seemed his nose would pull me toward him.

I yanked the starter cord of the canoe's motor. The blessed Honda fired and fell into idle. I shifted to reverse, thinking I could back away from him, but the canoe stood in place against the current, and water spilled over the square stern. I clunked the motor out of reverse and into forward, turning the canoe upstream in a wide arc, feeling the jerk of current when the canoe turned broadside.

Then I was motoring upstream in a 17-foot canoe, losing a race to a bear galloping through cottongrass like a thoroughbred. Twisting the throttle, I looked to my left and watched the bear, all rolling muscle and determination, just five yards of muddy water between us. He chased me upstream as he would a moose calf, and I wondered what I would do if he jumped in the water and torpedoed me.

He tore along the bank, pausing once to stand and sniff the air. For a few seconds, I felt the terror and exhilaration of a hunted animal.

As the bear and I raced upstream like a greyhound and a mechanical bunny, we came a wide spot where a slough oozed onto the river. The bear chose to go around the slough rather than swim across, giving me a buffer of 40 yards. I u-turned the canoe, holding my breath as the current whipped the bow downstream.

The bear stood, its front paws dropping at its side. My 8-horsepower motor and the seven-mile-per-hour push of the river were too much. I pulled away, looking back at the brown spot that disappeared as I rounded a bend.

The cabin was three miles downstream of the bear. As I reached the familiar mud-bar, I beached the canoe and reached for my .338 magnum, untying the loop of parachute cord that fastened it to the canoe. The gun was in my hands until I stepped inside the dark little cabin.

After making myself dinner, I called the Len on the two-way radio. A commander of men in Vietnam, Len knew what it felt like to be hunted by his own species, and he had once killed a bear that was rushing to kill him. He gave me advice to sleep on:

"If he starts ripping through that door, you just blow his shit away," Len said. "I have no problem with that."

With that, we said goodnight. I clicked off the radio, its hiss dying a few seconds later. My ears became tuned to silence. Intermittent drops of rain on the metal roof sped my heart a few beats.

In the privileged world in which I live, there's not much to fear. No one is trying to kill me; I can survive with my senses at half power. This bear probably does not want to kill me, but I know he's stronger than me, faster than me, and he can detect my presence long before I can his. What did he want out there on the river? Did he think I was a swimming moose, about to stumble though wet mud on his side of the river? Did my scent remind him of the maple syrup he sampled at the cabin?

The bear has ground the dull edge off my senses. I can't shake the image of his round, determined face, of his eyes locked on the canoe, of teeth and claws ripping through plywood.

My fear is ridiculous. I could drop an elephant with the rifle leaning next to me. If Len were with me, I would not be scared at all. Being alone strips me of everything but me. I'm left with the wide eyes of a seven-year old trying to make sense of a night animal's shriek.

I set a flashlight by the bunk, its bulb pointing toward the door. I rehearse a mental routine—switch on the light, click off the safety, point the gun at the hole being ripped in the door, fire. Paranoid, for sure, but I can think of nothing else.

I light a candle. Its soft light shines through the south window of the cabin, touching the gnarled willows outside. I am alone in the middle of Alaska, waiting for a noise in the night.

RESPECT

Splayed flat on the snow like a toy soldier, I looked through the scope at the flickering ears of a caribou, bedded down 20 yards away. I sucked cool air into my lungs and puffed it out the side of my mouth, trying to control my heartbeat.

Minutes before, I had watched a group of caribou disappear behind a hill and, seeing my chance, had skied with a rifle slung over my back toward a hill where I thought they might appear next.

I guessed right. As I pawed my way up the knoll, I elevated my head slowly and saw three caribou looking the other way. I dropped back down and crawled like an iguana up the hill, getting so close that when I propped my rifle on my elbows one caribou's head almost filled my rifle scope.

Feeling the cold creeping into my legs, I waited a few uncomfortable minutes until the caribou leaned into the snow and pressed down to stand. I centered the crosshairs on the caribou's lower shoulder. One second later, the foothills of the Brooks Range absorbed the roar of a high-caliber rifle.

On that sunny late April day, I was trying to duplicate the success of my friend BJ, who had harvested a caribou the day before on the rolling snow dunes of the North Slope.

A few days earlier, BJ and I had followed the Dalton Highway 325 miles north on a day when breakup was wringing water out of Fairbanks. Driving through Atigun Pass, the division between Alaska's forested interior and the bumpy tablelands of the north slope, we returned to winter; the air temperature on the north side was 10 degrees F, the foothills were coated with knee-deep snow, and the sun was so brilliant it would cook the underside of our noses and force us to add duct tape side panels to our sunglasses.

With two other friends, we planned to ski off the Haul Road and past an invisible five-mile buffer to hunt for spring caribou. The latitude we traversed on the drive was like gaining altitude. The naked landscape and the bite of the sun made it seem as if we were at 14,000 feet on Denali, but our tent camp would be no higher than the hills surrounding Fairbanks.

I shared a tent with BJ, who had volunteered to drive us north in his battered Toyota Corona wagon, its hood held down by a bungee cord. Though I hadn't hunted with him before, I remembered watching his leggy strides up a hill on skis during a wilderness race and getting bogged down trying to follow him; I once watched him strip my truck engine to bare pistons, then put it back together. The truck started when I turned the key.

On the long drive north, BJ nodded with enthusiasm about the possibility of harvesting a caribou.

"I've been thinking about this for months," he said. "I can't wait to get out there."

I felt a twinge about the way I had left Fairbanks, stuffing gear and food into my pack after finishing a hut-to-hut ski trip less than one week before. As we drove north over hills of twisted black spruce, I thought of binoculars, ski skins and other items I'd forgotten.

On our second day in, BJ spotted the first caribou on a hillside—antlerless animals walking single file like camels in a far-north desert. Watching their deliberate progress, I thought of them surviving dark, cold nights of 70 below windchills, dodging hungry wolves and enduring parasitic warble flies that drill beneath their winter coats. And here we came, after spending those cold nights behind insulated walls, with devices that hurled lead hundreds of yards.

After our first night outside, thoughts of meat in the freezer overwhelmed my sympathetic leanings. Within two days, BJ had stalked a lean bull and shot it from 300 paces. His 30-06 rifle had a peep sight—a rear plate with a tiny hole in it through which a shooter centers a front pin. Longer shots can be tricky with a peep sight, but in anticipation of the trip BJ had shot several boxes of shells through his gun.

Which brings the story back to me, belly-down in the snow, smoke curling from the barrel of my .338 magnum.

After the shot, I stood on stiff legs and began punching my way in ski boots up the hill to the caribou's body. But there was no body. The caribou had vanished, and the snow was white except for a few urine stains.

"No way," I said to myself, "There's no way I missed from that close."

Movement far away caught my eye—a Chilkoot-Trail scene of caribou in procession, climbing a hill. When I first saw them, I had counted eight. As they came into view one by one, I counted the caribou again.

"Six . . . seven . . . eight!"

The last few caribou seemed as nimble as the first, showing no sign of being nicked. As they melted over a mountain, I followed their trail, wondering how I missed a 20-yard shot.

We solved the mystery the next day, when BJ threaded a freeze-dried dinner wrapper though a willow branch and I aimed for the little hikers on the label. My shots cleared the hikers by several inches.

I wasn't always that careless. When I was 16, I hunted grouse and deer the way the other boys chased girls. I subscribed to Outdoor Life and spent every weekend and the daylight hours after school with a rifle or shotgun in my hands. I have forgotten a lot about hunting since then, but I still know sighting in a rifle before every hunt is a debt you owe the animals. On this trip, in my rush to get out the door, I didn't get to the rifle range.

Wrapped in my sleeping bag later that night, the thought that poked at my brain was how disgusted the 16-year old version of me would have been at the 40-year old. I had shown disrespect for the animals, and my human partners, who would have helped chase a wounded animal.

Looking over at body curled in the sleeping bag next to me, I pictured BJ at the rifle range on a 10 below Fairbanks morning, pushing shells into his gun with cold fingers. Then I thought of the caribou meat he had stored in snow pit nearby. BJ said his shot was a long one, but his brace was good and, most importantly, he had practiced with his gun from that range. He had taken care of all he could control in an unpredictable situation, something I had failed to do.

Identifying my mistake didn't make it any easier to sleep that night, but I made a few changes after we got home—I got rid of my big rifle, the one a hunting-guide boss once recommended for bears in thick brush, the one that punched my shoulder so hard that I hated sighting it in. I traded it for a gun that shoots smaller bullets and uses a lot less powder to push them. Before I brought it home, I took the gun to the Fairbanks rifle range, down by the dump, and shot it until heat waves curled from the barrel. Then I waited for the metal to cool down, and shot again.

COOL SCHOOL

The last time I walked into this building, I was 19 years old, two stripes hung on my sleeves, and a doctor was looking at the blackened tips of my fingers. I was new to Alaska and to 30 below, and had skied for too long wearing gloves instead of mittens. My frostbitten fingertips swelled like olives before deflating and turning purple and black, gross enough that a photo of them appeared in the Goldpanner, the Eielson Air Force Base newspaper.

Twenty-one years later, I'm back at Eielson at the invite of Air Force major Guyan Mandich, commander of the "Cool School." In business since 1947, the Air Force's Arctic Survival School has graduated hundreds of military fliers who might someday find themselves shot down in a cold, sparse place that resembles Interior Alaska.

Major Mandich allowed me to take the weeklong course as the only civilian. After the two days in the classroom, 31 military fliers and I would depart for the woods behind base with flight bags that each contained a large knife, a can of pork and beans, and two MREs (Meals, Ready to Eat). That's not many calories for three days, but we would try to supplement other meals in the boreal forest.

"This is a U.S. Air Force Arctic Survival School," an instructor said during a class. "We kill things here."

A blue bus picked us up on Wednesday morning to take us to the training site, in the hills about six behind the base. It wouldn't return for us until Friday afternoon, when our training would be complete. As the bus rumbled along, I thought of the many buses I'd ridden during my four-year hitch in the Air Force, including one that would, for a buck, take car-less airmen like me 30 miles from Eielson to Fairbanks.

OK, no more memories. I was at Eielson in early March to see what I could learn about surviving in the cold. During ski trips across frozen sections of Alaska, my friends and I stay alive with constant movement while carrying light packs or sleds. During the survival course, the instructors made us pack flight bags with about 60 pounds of gear, not including the bunny boots most of us wore. We were simulating what you'd have if your plane wrecked but you crawled out, dragging your stuff with you.

The first thing we did as a group was build a fire, throwing on logs that a firewood contractor had hauled into the training site months before (to use local trees would have deforested the training area long ago). I never make campfires in Alaska, mostly because my method of travel—hiking or skiing usually—makes me too tired to go through the effort of gathering wood.

Our young instructors—twenty-somethings Airman Jason Clapper and Sergeant Sean Hanson, who had both been in Alaska just a few years—had us pull out our large knives to start the training. They taught us how to take down a tree with those knives. Then we split logs with the knives, and used them to feather those logs into kindling.

The second thing they taught us was how to make snares out of safety wire, secure those snares to drag sticks, and set them in the paths of snowshoe hares.

"You're going to get pretty hungry in a few days," Clapper said. "You'll be less hungry if you can get some meat."

In early March, the midday sun was beginning to get some punch and the forecast was for lows of ten below zero. A class before us had slept in their snow shelters at 40 below; we, they said, would have it easy.

"You should get asterisks on your graduation certificates," one instructor said.

Clapper taught us how to build a "thermal A-frame shelter," which consisted of a frame of thin logs covered with a parachute, smothered by snow. The floor of a thermal A-frame is grass or tundra, scraped clean of snow.

"This way you use the heat of the ground along with the insulation of the snow covering the shelter," Clapper said. "You should stay about 18-to-22 degrees no matter how cold it is outside."

I had a way to check that, having brought along a few temperature probes. Every 20 minutes, the probes measured the temperature of the outside air and the inside air.

After I built my shelter but before I crawled in, the temperature inside was 20 degrees while the outside air was 15.

When I squeezed through the entry hole at 9 p.m. and pulled the door plug behind me, the temperature inside climbed at 29 degrees and stayed there all night, even when the outside temperature dropped to minus 1.

I remember a warm, quiet night inside that shelter, and I remember being thankful for the plastic "Piddle Pak" airman Shane Leary gave me before I went in. Because of his generosity, I didn't need to push out my door plug during the night. A few weeks after class, airman Leary emailed me, saying it was nice meeting me and that he was headed to Iraq for a year.

Most of my classmates had served in the Middle East, and all of them had spent long tours overseas. During our hours around the campfire during the night, my nine comrades had stories from every continent except Antarctica and South America. It sounded a lot more exciting than my four years during the Reagan Cold War era, with a lot higher stakes.

By Friday morning, most of us had eaten everything in our MRE packets. The pork and beans were a distant memory. The hares had avoided our traps, and we knocked back stomach pangs by chugging smoke-flavored water. Seeing that our snares weren't producing, Clapper showed up at first light with a red squirrel in his hand.

He'd taken the tiny creature with a homemade slingshot, and the 27-year old skinned and quartered it with a jackknife before tossing the edibles into a tin coffee can of boiling water.

Split 10 ways, a red squirrel doesn't go far. Clapper stirred seasonings into the pot with a stick. After the stew boiled, we passed the can around and took sips. A few gnawed on meat from miniature bones. On my sip, I felt the squirrel's liver pass my lips. I swallowed it down. I wished I had another.

After we finished our squirrel, we cleaned up and prepared to go back to pre-ordered submarine sandwiches and the rest of our lives. On the bus ride out of the hills, I thought back to the past few days and what those young newcomers like Airman Clapper had, if anything, to teach me.

Answer: A lot. These guys were pros, and what they lacked in sourdough status they made up for in enthusiasm and skill. Clapper once lit a fire by sparking a magnesium stick with his knife blade over birch bark, a trick that took me half a day. I was the slowest student at almost everything, from constructing a shelter to making fires from scratch. And I'm still trying to forget who earned the red lantern in the sharpest-knife contest.

When it was over, Major Mandich gave me a Cool School medallion, invited me back to ski on their snowcat trails, and even let me take a shower in the headquarters before I left. Later, I drove off base beneath jets roaring off the flightline and thought of the jockeys within them. Then I passed the gates, hit the Richardson Highway and returned to my wife, my dogs and a life that doesn't include a mandatory trip to Iraq or Afghanistan.

SOUTHEAST RISING

My favorite earthquake struck during one of my first camping trips in Alaska. I had just unrolled my thin foam pad over the powdered soil of an interior Alaska hilltop and was lying belly-down when the ground moved down, then up, as if I had done a pushup. The power of the Earth rolled through my body, from the tips of my toes to my elbows. I was then a 19-year old airman camping in the hills above Eielson Air Force Base, and I have not felt the Earth speak as sharply since.

I am now straining to feel the Earth move again. I know this island is rising faster than most anywhere on the planet, and I'm trying to feel a slow push to the sky. So far, my senses are too dull to pick up the movement, and it's hard to filter out the stirrings of Chris Larsen and Adam Bucki, the other bodies inside this three-man tent.

We are camped on Cenotaph Island in Lituya Bay, on the west side of Glacier Bay National Park near the open Pacific. Our weeklong mission here is to measure a force called glacial rebound at one of the spots where the ground is springing upward with the most gusto. Southeast will probably continue rising for another seven centuries, says Chris, an expert on these matters.

Of course, fast to a geologist is pretty slow to the rest of us. The island on which we camp is rising about one-half inch each year, which means our campsite will be four feet higher in a century. The driving force behind the elevation gain is one of the most dramatic ice losses the modern world has seen.

In 1794, just after Americans had reelected George Washington to his second term, British explorer George Vancouver saw a calving wall of ice at what is now the entrance to Glacier Bay. Since then, a chunk of ice more than 60 miles long and almost one mile high has disappeared from Glacier Bay. Spread the former ice of Glacier Bay over Alaska, and every inch of the state would be buried seven feet under an icecap.

"That melting happened in only a few hundred years," Chris says over morning coffee on a Cenotaph Island beach. "About 2,500 cubic kilometers of ice melted there, and a single cubic kilometer of ice weighs about as much as 10,000 Nimitz-class aircraft carriers. It's insane."

The removal of 25 million aircraft carriers from the property is bound to affect the foundation. Chris thinks that weight loss is making southeast Alaska the fastest-rising place on Earth, heading toward the clouds even faster than the Himalayas. The ground is rising here because Earth's crust is floating on a molten inner layer, and the liberation from beneath that load is causing the surface to bounce back. We are setting up super-accurate GPS receivers around Lituya Bay, about 30 miles west of Glacier Bay, to determine the speed of the rebound. Chris, Adam, and others have traveled throughout southeast Alaska doing the same thing.

Glacial rebound is happening other places in the world, though not as fast as in Southeast. A massive shield of ice melted about 10,000 years ago in northern Canada, leaving behind Hudson Bay. Land surrounding the bay has risen 350 feet since then. Looking back at tree-ring records of former shorelines, Chris and his coworkers have found that rocky shorelines along Lynn Canal have risen more than 18 feet since George Vancouver sailed by.

Chris is trying to clock the speed at which areas of Southeast are rebounding by measuring the elevation of same points that he and other scientists have measured several times in the past five years. We are setting up global positioning system receivers on sturdy tripods at several shoreline rock formations here within Lituya Bay. The receivers perform the same function as hand-held GPS units, but these are roughly the size of laptop computers, accurate to the thickness of two dimes, and cost more than a new snowmachine.

After breakfast, we each heave on a handle of a beached Zodiac and stagger it to tide line. We motor out into the bay, the wooden floor platform of the vinyl boat cluttered with batteries, receivers, and other parts. Adam revs up the outboard and points the Zodiac toward a hut-size rock on the northern shore. As we get closer, we notice the equipment is not as neat as it was when we installed it the day before—a yellow nylon bag that protected the receiver yawns on the beach, and coax cable spills over the shoreline like spaghetti.

A bear has yanked the GPS receiver off the rock and snuffled through the various components, snipping through one of the coax cables. Chris spends a few minutes repairing the cable with his Swiss Army knife and a roll of electrical tape.

As he works, the mountains of the Fairweather Range shoulder through the clouds, and the glory of Lituya Bay reveals itself. Mt. Crillon juts 12,726 feet into the sky less than 15 miles from the ocean. Three different glaciers stick their cold tongues toward the bay. Minty-smelling stands of cottonwood perfume the salt air and tell a story; the trees have all germinated since 1958, when a massive earthquake shook a good portion of a nearby mountain into the water, causing a wave 10 stories tall to rip through the bay at 100 miles per hour. The giant earthquake happened because the Fairweather fault, a weak point in Earth's crust, slashes though the back of the bay, creating the trench filled with two of the bay's glaciers. Adding to the mystique of the bay is its narrow entrance to the ocean a few miles west of us. Tidal currents push and pull vast amounts of salt water through the gap, which is almost tight enough to throw a rock across. Twenty-one French explorers died there during a few terrible minutes in 1786.

The roar of the ocean and the sight of new trees that replaced the ones eaten by the giant wave are the immediate distractions in Lituya Bay; the notion that this place is rising faster than anywhere else on the planet is just that, an intellectual concept detected by satellite and computer, out of the range of human senses. As hard as I try during these still nights on Cenotaph Island, I can't feel the ground shoving us toward the stars.

Those of us who don't own ever-expanding waterfront golf courses in Gustavus will probably never notice the rise of southeast Alaska, but scientists like Chris care about it because removing an immense weight from an area is bound to change to the stresses within Earth's crust that cause earthquakes.

As for me, I like the idea of my adopted home having another superlative attached to its name—*the fastest rising place on Earth*. And I like getting to know more about this place. The more I learn, the more interesting Alaska becomes, and the more I want to roll my sleeping pad over its surface, let the noises of the day drain away, and listen.

THE BEAR MAGNET

She describes herself as a "bear magnet." It's hard to argue with that.

Two days after we married, Kristen and I took a backpacking trip in New York's Adirondack Mountains. Our second night out, a black bear prowled around our open lean-to as we cooked dinner. The large blackie kept us awake all night by batting our bear-proof container around the forest; our dog Chloe growled at the moving shadow for hours. I had spent my first 18 years in upstate New York. I'd never even seen a bear track before that trip with Kristen.

There was another time, on a hike on the Goat Trail through the Wrangell Mountains. It was one of our first hikes together, and Kristen insisted we carry a shotgun along for bear protection. With anyone else I would have spouted about the astronomically low chances of us running into a dangerous bear. But, because Kristen was hiking with me, I shut up and carried the shotgun. And, as we were hiking to a wade-able part of the Chitistone River, a black bear was ambling toward the same crossing; he seemed to be racing to meet us there. As we let him pass, he gave a few sideways glances. The seven pounds of shotgun I was carrying didn't feel so heavy then.

In the year when I heard Kristen's name on the radio, I carried that shotgun for 800 miles, all the way across Alaska, when I hiked from Valdez to Prudhoe Bay with my dog. I thought differently about bears then; I carried a lot more fear than I do now. But that 120-day trip, free of any dicey bear encounters, made me see as minimal the risks of death by bear. Take care of your food, make noise, and you have no problems.

Since that hike, nine years ago, I've bumped into several bears, including a grizzly family feeding on a moose, but I've been lucky enough to come back with nothing but stories. Bear encounters have slipped way down on my list of things that could go wrong out there.

Bear encounters are still up there on Kristen's list. Not too long ago, she would wake at the slightest noise outside the tent, and she'd wake me up, too.

"Did you hear that?" she'd say, sitting up in her sleeping bag.

I'd listen, then go back to sleep because my brain doesn't hold the images that hers does. Like the one of a grizzly pushing your face into the forest floor.

I met Kristen at a running race. A former girlfriend of mine introduced us, and I learned that Kristen was a bird biologist who had spent the previous summer working in the forest near the McCarthy Road. I thought back to the radio report I'd heard while I was walking the pipeline.

"Did you know that biologist who was attacked by the bear out there?" I asked.

"That was me," she said, quietly, before changing the subject.

She's such a lighthearted person, with a smile being the default mode to which her face always returns, that it's easy to forget that she has undergone such a trauma dealt by a wild animal. And her fight to overcome her phobia of camping has been a success; there now seems to be little residue of fear when she rolls out her sleeping bag for the night. You couldn't blame someone like her if she never ventured near wild places again. But Kristen jumped right back in.

And she has the best bear story I've ever heard someone tell, but she only gives it up when prompted.

The last time she told the bear story was one of the most memorable. She was in the hospital in Fairbanks, and had been up all night with teeth-grinding contractions so painful she couldn't speak. After more than 12 hours of enduring a new mother's agony, she nodded with vigor to the doctor when he suggested an epidural, anesthesia that would numb her from the waist down.

She endured another excruciating hour of contractions before the anesthesiologist, who was busy with a C-section in another room, arrived. Practiced in his craft, the anesthesiologist distracted her with small talk about things other than childbirth when he noticed something to ask her about.

"Where'd you get these scars on your shoulder and back?"

Just then, the drug kicked in, and Kristen regained the ability to speak. There, in a hospital room, at four a.m. on a Tuesday, she told her story.

The anesthesiologist's eyes widened as he heard of a charging grizzly that didn't stop after getting a muzzle full of pepper spray. The doctor and medical student observing at bedside weren't so sleepy anymore when they heard about how the bear knocked Kristen down, clawed her back and the rear of her head, and bit through her wristwatch. And her wrist.

They stood there at that sleepy hour as Kristen described how she tried to crawl away after the initial attack, then felt the bear whack her back to the ground. That's when, using its jaws, it pinned her head to the ground, and she thought her time had come.

In the quiet of the Women's Center at Fairbanks Memorial Hospital, the medical folks listened when Kristen described how the bear eventually left her alone, and how after what felt like an eternity she crawled and walked out to the McCarthy Road, where her coworker picked her up and drove her to Glennallen. There, doctors cleaned and stitched up her wounds and wondered aloud how lucky she was.

Now, nine years later and about 10 hours after the anesthesiologist left the room with a new story, Kristen and I felt as lucky as we ever have. After several hours of athletic effort, she pushed into the world a nine-pound, two-ounce little girl with a full head of hair.

Anna Kay Rozell has her Mom's long fingers, her nose, and curvy toes that will someday press deep into the tundra. I hope she also was fortunate enough to inherit her mother's sunny nature and resilience. Little A.K. will someday learn about her Mom's unique qualities. Maybe it'll be when she's nine or 10, and she notices those scars on her mommy's back and shoulders, and she hears the bear story for the first time.

89042466R00085

Made in the USA
Columbia, SC
17 February 2018